The
Leisure Environment

Rosalyn Doggett

and

Rose O'Mahoney

Stanley Thornes (Publishers) Ltd

First published in 1991 by:
Stanley Thornes (Publishers) Ltd
Old Station Drive
Leckhampton
CHELTENHAM GL53 0DN
England

British Library Cataloguing in Publication Data

Doggett, Rosalyn
    The leisure environment.
    I. Title   II. O'Mahoney, Rose
    790.01

    ISBN 0–7487–0416–7

Typeset by Tech-Set, Gateshead, Tyne & Wear.
Printed and bound in Great Britain at The Bath Press, Avon.

The Leisure Environment

Also published by Stanley Thornes (Publishers) Ltd

For BTEC First Certificate in Business and Finance:

Joseph Chilver, *Introduction to Financial Calculations*

For BTEC National Diploma in Business and Finance

Don Robinson, *et al.*, *People in Organisations*
Joseph Chilver, *Finance*
Gillian Dale, *The Business of Retailing*

Dedication

To the epitome of leisure!

RAD

To Dad and Mum

RO'M

Acknowledgements

Rosalyn Doggett would like to thank Dr Neil Burgess for his technical assistance, inspiration and patience, and Tobias for the opportunity to finish this book.

The authors would also like to thank Noel Kavanagh, Gillian Dale, John Wyett (for the financial information in Assignment 12), Hilary Allison (former Regional Information Officer, National Trust East Anglia Region) and students at Cambridge Regional College who have tried and tested (perhaps unwittingly) the activities and assignments.

The authors and publishers would like to thank the following for permission to reproduce material:

Arts Council, p. 42 ● Avon Ski Centre, p. 63 ● Barnaby's Picture Library, p. 18 ● Mr R. Boyd and Mr P. Barringer, p. 59 (*Milton Village Voice*) ● CACI, p. 94 ● CCPR, p. 43 ● *Cambridge Evening News*, p. 75 ● Cheltenham Tourism, p. 52 ● Embassy Hotels, p. 153 ● *East Cambridgeshire Town Crier*, p. 57 ● Falcon Sailing, p. 103 ● Girl Guides Association, p. 158 ● Gloucestershire County Council, p. 53 ● Grafham Water Reservoir, p. 99 ● Great Yarmouth Marina, p. 122 ● *The Guardian*, pp. 17, 158–9 ● Health Education Authority (LAYH Project Centre), p. 140 (photograph © The Post Office) ● The Junction, Cambridge, p. 9 ● *Leisure Management*, pp. 101, 102* ● A.T. Mays, p. 5 ● Mecca Leisure Ltd, pp. 27, 35 ● Merseyside Photo Library, p. 124 ● National Museum of Photography, Film and Television, p. 128 ● National Trust, pp. 14, 77–83 ● Newent Community School, Gloucestershire, p. 56 ● Oasis Leisure Centre, Swindon, p. 32 ● Popperfoto, p. 2 ● Ridings Shopping Centre, Wakefield, p. 126 ● Sports Council, pp. 43, 160–3 ● *Sports and Leisure* magazine, pp. 33, 40, 62 ● Wildfowl and Wetlands Trust, p. 3.

*Tables of statistics are reproduced with the permission of the Central Statistical Office, the Office of Population Censuses and Surveys, and HMSO, © Crown.

Every effort has been made to contact copyright holders, and we apologise if any have been overlooked.

Contents

14 Design 152
Principles of good design ● Outdoor leisure facilities ● Corporate image ● Assignment 15: Design a leisure centre

Preface

The Leisure Environment seeks to provide an overview of the expanding leisure industry. The emphasis is vocational and there is a combination of text, case studies, role plays and student-centred activities. *The Leisure Environment* starts with an historical perspective, followed by a detailed practical analysis of the structure, size and scope of the leisure industry, and a profile of the people who use it. Management and marketing functions are also introduced.

For students seeking employment in leisure the chapter on managing and planning leisure emphasises the diverse nature of the industry and provides useful sources of further information. An examination of the international scene looks at outside influences on the development of the industry in the UK. The text follows the requirements of the BTEC National Diploma in Leisure core syllabus 'The Leisure Environment' and will be a useful resource for BTEC First Certificate and Open Learning students. It can also be used as a foundation textbook for leisure students in higher education.

Rosalyn Ann Doggett
Rose O'Mahoney
1991

What is leisure?

Aims

▶ To define the meaning of leisure
▶ To discover what leisure time means to different people in society
▶ To compare different leisure activities
▶ To introduce the importance of leisure today

Leisure time

I became interested in the idea that the country was becoming a theme park, and puzzled by the decline in manufacture, the disappearance of mass employment and the rise of leisure.

From 'Time to stop and stare' by Martin Corrick,
The Guardian, 9 February 1990

A dictionary definition of the word 'leisure' states that this is 'time at one's own disposal' but this only goes a little way into describing what 'leisure' actually means to everyone. If you think of your own situation, leisure time may mean the time when you can do as you choose. To someone at school this may mean the time after the bell rings at the end of the lesson signalling a break in the day's formal activities or lessons. This time might be spent sitting and talking with friends, or just kicking or throwing a ball around – really just doing what you want to within certain time limits.

For a person at home all day, leisure time might be the time spent sitting in a favourite armchair relaxing, having completed all the domestic chores. Therefore leisure can be the time used at a person's own discretion in a variety of ways, once they have completed certain obligations like study, domestic chores or work, i.e. the time left over or residual time.

Leisure in society

Certain interests, hobbies and sports are seen by people in society as a 'constructive' use of leisure, and as such they perform a useful function. A constructive use of leisure may be learning a skill such as dressmaking or another language, or being more physically active by swimming or playing sport, or searching out and collecting various items like stamps or antiques.

If you undertake these activities you will learn skills and gain knowledge which will be useful to your own personal development. The people who have these interests are more able to 'fit in' with others in the society in which they live. They mix with others with similar interests and develop social skills.

Freedom and leisure

Many people wish they had more free time to pursue leisure interests and activities. However we have to ask ourselves if we are really free to choose? One form of control is through laws which restrict us from undertaking certain activities which society believes are a bad or a vulgar use of leisure time. For example, dog fighting or cock fighting is illegal in the UK, and is considered a socially unacceptable use of leisure time.

As an individual in society you are conditioned or taught that certain leisure pursuits are desirable and good, whereas others are unnecessary and not encouraged. In addition to this there is pressure from colleagues and friends which has a direct effect on our leisure pursuits. There are also other external influences such as fashion or trends (both within this country and from abroad) that influence our leisure time and activities. These influences are discussed in more detail in Chapter 2.

Leisure activities

Now with your available time you can pursue some leisure activity. This can be a passive activity which involves very little physical effort such as relaxing, watching television, listening to the radio or to music. Alternatively it can be an active pursuit such as playing sport, dancing, or aerobics, all needing physical movement and effort.

However, a moment's thought would soon remind you that, in leisure terms, the majority of activities undertaken are combinations of both passive activities and active pursuits. For example, going on holiday could be categorised as an active pursuit, but although you may actively travel to your destination (perhaps by cycling) you may then spend the majority of the time lying on a beach sunbathing, which is a passive activity!

The range and diversity of leisure interests are very wide and may include the following:

Home-based

These can be passive or active, such as watching television and videos, knitting, listening to music, reading, writing, gardening, do-it-yourself or home maintenance.

Educational and cultural

These can take the form of enrolling for further education classes, learning new skills such as ballroom dancing or languages, going to the theatre, the opera, or ballet, visiting museums, art galleries or taking part in cultural holidays at home or abroad.

▲ *The Tennis Championships at Wimbledon: a popular spectator event and participant sport*

Sporting

These can be spontaneous activities which cost nothing and which you can pursue with a group of friends in the area where you live, e.g. playing ball in the garden at home, or jogging in the park. Alternatively they can be more formalised activities 'sold' to you by the commercial or business world. If you 'buy' into these activities then you pay for entrance into the venue and expect a certain standard of facilities in return – visiting the local swimming pool or badminton courts, for example. A person can either participate in these sporting activities or watch them.

These are referred to as either **participation sports**, such as playing football, hockey, or rowing, or **spectator sports**, such as watching snooker matches, rugby games or tennis matches.

Social and caring

Social leisure activities can involve the commercial world (i.e. buying into them) – for example, eating out, drinking, visiting cinemas, gambling, dancing, holidaying – but can also involve home entertainment such as arranging dinner parties or just having friends around for drinks.

For some people running a charity stall at a local market, undertaking hospital visiting, or being involved in fund raising events for a worthy cause is a constructive use of their leisure time.

Nature and environmental

Often people find a great deal of enjoyment pursuing spontaneous activities that cost them very little in financial terms and that they arrange themselves, such as bird watching, walking or rambling, camping and caravanning. Various clubs and societies have been established in order to bring together people with these interests, for example, the Royal Society for the Protection of Birds (RSPB) for those interested in bird life and nature, The National Trust, local Wildlife Groups, the Youth Hostel Association, the Caravan Club and so on.

Pressure groups for environmental protection, such as Friends of the Earth or Greenpeace, attract people who use their leisure time to become actively involved in these groups' activities against pollution of the environment and for the protection of wildlife.

▲ *Birdwatching: an outdoor activity. Twitchers often travel long distances to see unusual birds*

Leisure as play

The majority of people would state that they undertake leisure activities for fun, or not for serious purposes. This contrasts with most other obligations or activities in life which have a serious side to them, such as working to earn money, or household chores. Because leisure activities can be described as play there is no obligation to complete them. A person should enjoy their leisure activities. However, many games and activities have complex or special rules and in order to join in a person must learn the rules. These rules mark the boundaries of play.

Three main types of play
1 Games of skill
2 Games of chance
3 Escapism

Some activities demand great skill and dexterity, such as playing chess or tennis, whereas others are games of chance, such as bingo or other forms of gambling. Other games demand taking on a different personality and are based on escapism or make-believe – 'Dungeons and Dragons', for instance.

ACTIVITY

Think about your leisure activities in terms of play and ask yourself the following questions:

1 Do your leisure activities demand skill? If so what are these activities and what type of skills do they need? Make a list of these.

2 Do you undertake any leisure activities which are based purely on chance or luck?

3 Think back to when you were a child. What games did you play that fall into the escapist category?

If people use their leisure time to undertake play activities then it is seen by some academics as having a function in developing social skills, stimulating behaviour, aiding educational development and so on. If you think about how young children learn social skills through playing with toys or make-believe games, then you can understand how this theory might also apply to adults.

It is thought that there is a basic instinct to motivate us to play in order to relieve the stresses and strains of our other obligations. Those people who are very good at games of skill may well be compensating for lack of ability in other areas of their life. Sometimes this results in taking these leisure activities too seriously; games become too competitive and the sense of fun or enjoyment is lost.

Work and leisure

'Work' describes many types of activities, as well as the stereotyped idea of paid employment. 'Work' can be any of the following:

- Domestic chores
- Caring for children in the home
- Voluntary work
- Study time
- Self-employment
- Working for an employer.

These are all obligations on an individual's time, whether they are done by choice or necessity, and as such they reduce the amount of leisure time.

Whether you live in the sophisticated western world or a developing country you will have to adopt a certain discipline of living, involving activities that cannot be ignored. For instance, planting crops in an agricultural society is defined as 'work' for those people involved, as is hunting and fishing, as these chores have to be accomplished in order to live.

Unemployment

Looking at 'work' in this broad sense makes it easier to understand the concept of people who are 'unemployed' in western societies. They are unemployed in that they undertake no paid employment, but they have certain obligations they have to fulfil in the home environment before they can follow their leisure interests. If you agree with this statement you can see that someone who is technically 'out of work' does not necessarily have a vast unlimited amount of leisure time with no prior calls on that time, although they may well have more leisure time than someone who undertakes paid employment outside the home.

Paid employment

The main difference between those who have paid employment and those who work in other ways, is that a person with paid employment has generally more money to spend on their leisure activities than a person who has no formal paid employment.

Time for leisure

Another essential difference is working hours. People with no paid employment can usually choose when they complete their tasks. If you have a full-time paid job of work outside the home in the UK you may work 37 to 40 hours, as a standard working week. Your hours may well be the 'normal' or standard working day, normally 9 a.m. to 5 p.m., with a one hour lunchbreak. However, there are many variations on this, such as flexitime (choosing your own work hours within certain time bands), shift work, three-day weeks, ten-day work periods, job shares and so on. Obviously work patterns are affected by the job you complete (compare a factory operative's work pattern with a shop sales assistant's) and therefore the time you spend at leisure.

Location

Where you live has a direct influence on paid work and therefore leisure. In the UK many small towns have a closing day mid-week to compensate for Saturday working in the retail trade, and Sunday hours of work also have to be compensated for by time off later in the week or month.

If you live and work in a country such as Spain, which has a hot climate, you will find the standard working hours split into two sections throughout the day; the first in the morning, followed by a long break or 'siesta', and the second in the late afternoon and early evening. Countries all over the world have vastly different standards for paid working hours depending on climate (it may be too hot or too cold to work at certain times), geography of the area (it may be too remote to need strict routines), the nature of the people, the culture and religious teaching.

Whatever type of work you undertake, the amount of physical and mental effort and energy it consumes will dictate how much energy and motivation you have left over for leisure activities.

In a very formal type of work situation, such as some types of paid employment, workers may have to be very disciplined, for example, they must arrive at a fixed time and complete certain tasks within time limits; these could be extremely tedious or boring routines. These workers' leisure activities may be a direct contrast to their work activities, involving informal or spontaneous activities such as listening to music, drinking at the local pub, or watching television.

In some forms of paid employment leisure activity is encouraged; workers can socialise in order to enhance business relations between companies – for example, inter-company league squash matches. Leisure activities may be undertaken with business clients; for example, a salesperson may play golf during working hours with a potential customer. This puts the customer at ease in a social situation, making it easier for the worker to negotiate a contract.

In summary, therefore, work means many things to different people. It is not enough to restrict the idea of work to paid employment outside the home, and it is clear that a person's available leisure time and motivation for leisure activities can vary considerably, depending on the work they do.

Sources of information

To study any subject you must find and use a range of sources of information to make sense of the subject details. Leisure is a growing industry in our post-industrial society and therefore an increasing amount of research is being undertaken in the study of leisure. Within the following chapters a range of different sources of information are consulted and you will be guided to many others.

The most comprehensive sources of information on the leisure industry are the government surveys which are compiled by the Central Statistical Office (CSO) and printed by Her Majesty's Stationery Office (HMSO). The government monitors and collates information about the way people spend their time, and their standards of living: for example, the General Household Survey, Social Trends, Regional Trends and the Family Expenditure Survey.

Table 1.1 Social activities and hobbies: participation rates in the four weeks before interview by age, for men and for women

Persons aged 16 and over   *Great Britain: 1986*

Social activities and hobbies – on prompt list**	Age								Median age of adult participants
	16–19	20–24	25–29	30–44	45–59	60–69	70 or over	Total	
Men			Percentage participating in the 4 weeks before interview						
Visiting/entertaining friends/relations	94	96	96	94	91	91	86	92	42
Going out for a meal	41	56	57	52	48	39	31	47	40
Going out for a drink	71	89	84	73	61	50	30	65	38
Watching TV	99	99	98	99	98	98	96	98	43
Listening to radio	94	93	91	90	85	83	77	87	42
Listening to records/tapes	96	91	86	77	63	50	33	69	38
Reading books	46	48	51	55	52	55	49	52	43
Gardening	19	22	38	51	58	59	51	47	48
DIY	29	43	61	67	60	51	29	54	42
Dressmaking/needlework/knitting	4	3	4	3	3	3	3	3	41
Total – at least one activity	100	100	100	100	100	100	100	100	43
Base = 100%	*704*	*795*	*816*	*2499*	*1910*	*1191*	*976*	*8891*	*43*
Women									
Visiting/entertaining friends/relations	97	98	98	96	95	94	91	95	44
Going out for a meal	50	59	55	52	50	40	30	47	41
Going out for a drink	72	82	65	58	43	26	11	47	36
Watching TV	99	99	99	99	99	98	97	98	44
Listening to radio	96	94	88	87	84	81	73	85	43
Listening to records/tapes	96	91	84	77	61	45	25	65	38
Reading books	68	64	65	67	64	64	60	64	44
Gardening	9	19	36	47	47	45	33	39	47
DIY	15	28	37	38	28	20	10	27	40
Dressmaking/needlework/knitting	28	40	46	52	57	55	37	48	49
Total – at least one activity	100	100	100	100	100	100	100	100	44
Base = 100%	*674*	*884*	*957*	*2742*	*2013*	*1452*	*1596*	*10 318*	*44*

**These activities were on the prompt list and were therefore asked about specifically.

General Household Survey 1986.
Office of Population Censuses and Surveys, Social Survey Division HMSO (1989)

ACTIVITY

1 Men and women in various age groups were asked questions relating to their leisure interests (excluding sports activities) which occupied them in the four week period prior to the survey taking place. The percentages of men and women participating in activities was then calculated and broken down according to age. The results are shown in The General Household Survey for 1986, Table 1.1.
   a) Look at the figures in the first column (the 16 to 19 age group). What do these figures tell you about the book reading habits of men and women of this age?
   b) Think of some reasons for this behaviour. What are your conclusions?
   c) Choose another age group and activity and compare the percentages between men and women. What conclusions can you draw?

2 Carry out a mini survey amongst your friends, family and acquaintances. Find out:
   a) What types of leisure activity they undertake in their 'spare time'.
   b) Why they pursue their leisure pursuits. Make a list of their reasons.
   c) What changes they have noticed in the amount of leisure time they have available.
   d) Whether their leisure time has become more organised. If so, why? Use your findings for a group discussion.

Choices on how to use leisure time

The use of leisure time has interested many distinguished people in society; philosophers and social scientists have evolved theories as to why people use their leisure time as they do. One of these people, Nash, a philosopher and academic, formed the following theory.

The concept of a person's use of leisure time

According to Nash's philosophy of recreation and leisure, leisure activities are ranked according to their value to society. At the upper end of the scale he suggests that individuals use their leisure time for creative participation, composing music, inventing and so on. At the lower end of the scale people use their leisure time for delinquent acts and crime. However, each activity is not exclusive and a person could operate on several different levels during their leisure time.

Figure 1.1 illustrates this. Each person is given a numerical rating depending on their leisure interests; the higher the score the more creative they are and the person is considered more valuable to society. For example:

a) Person **A** is a heavy drinker, a gambler, and watches television. Rating: mostly 1.
b) Person **B** is a member of the football team, a squash player, writes novels and visits theatres. Rating: 3 and 4.

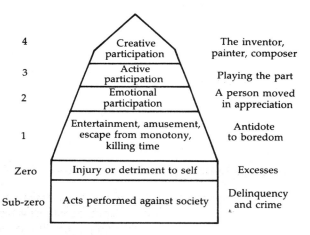

▲ *Figure 1.1   Nash's theory of leisure time*

Too many activities with a low rating are regarded as unhealthy, so the progress of personal development is much slower than a person who gets involved in higher-rated activities.

However, the theory has some flaws. For example, a person might be a brilliant professional writer, but leisure time is spent watching television (which according to the ratings scores only 1). This may be required as a form of escapism (see the section on play earlier in this chapter).

The theory is also based on the assumption that the more enjoyable and useful activities are more culturally based. Although Nash might have thought this was good, others might disagree. If you analyse your own activities closely, culture is not always a necessary goal in leisure time pursuits.

Reasons for recent growth in leisure activities

There are two main concepts, **demand** and **supply**, which have contributed to the growth of leisure activities, and have given the population a vast choice of what to do with their leisure time.

Demand

People have more time to fill when they are not committed to a form of work due to many labour and time-saving devices, and therefore they demand more leisure activities and interests. These leisure activities are varied, ranging from the spontaneous events that cost nothing (such as walking and rambling), to visiting a fun fair or a country house. People demand amusement and activity, for which they are prepared to venture outside the home, and in many cases they have income available to spend on these pursuits.

Supply

Business organisations now regard leisure activities as a necessity of the twentieth century and therefore seek to supply what they believe the public want. This includes opening sports and leisure centres and a vast array of leisure amenities that compete for customers. Business organisations also offer ancillary goods such as sports clothing and equipment, leisurewear, etc. to enhance the customers' enjoyment of leisure.

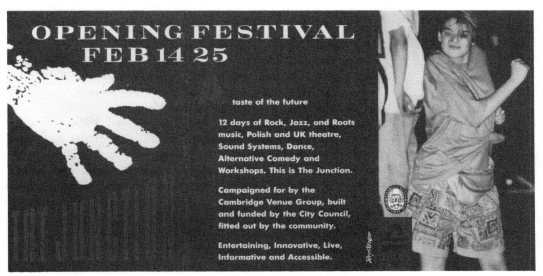

▲ *Publicity material for The Junction, Cambridge. This venue was campaigned for by the community*

Marketing has become an important part of the business. In many ways customers have their demands for leisure 'shaped' for them by business organisations that introduce and promote by advertising such things as amusement parks, arcades and fun fairs.

The growth in the range of leisure activities available has led to the formation of a **leisure industry** geared to the customer.

The industry is made up of:

1 The commercial business organisations selling services and goods, e.g. theme parks and sports shops
2 Government organisations providing amenities and services, e.g. local parks and gardens, swimming pools and cricket grounds
3 Various other organisations that do not fit neatly into the above two categories, e.g. youth clubs and various societies.

The trend, therefore, into the twenty-first century, is a further expansion in leisure and recreation provision, more sports centres, leisure and theme parks, cultural and education establishments and places for entertainment. It is suggested by those involved in the leisure industry that there will be greater opportunities for everyone to undertake a range of these pursuits and interests.

The leisure environment is growing and, as a service industry, will give scope for job opportunities. The popularity and diversity of the leisure environment might well improve the quality of life for many people and perhaps help them to be fitter, healthier and happier individuals.

/ACTIVITY/

Using the following classifications:

- Home-based activities
- Educational and cultural activities
- Sporting activities
- Social and caring activities
- Nature and environmental activities

1 Make a list of those leisure pursuits that you enjoy. Once the list is complete analyse each activity to find out if it is a passive or an active leisure pursuit.
2 Compare this list with that of another member of the group. How active are you?

Summary

▶ The leisure environment refers to the surroundings in which a person can pursue their interests, hobbies, recreation or sport.
▶ Leisure activities need available time which is not allocated to any other form of activity.
▶ Leisure activities can be passive or active, or a mixture of both.
▶ Leisure activities vary from person to person depending on many factors to do with a person's home life, and where and how he or she lives. These activities can be categorised in different groups: home-based, educational and cultural, sport, social and caring, and nature and environmental.
▶ In general people are free to choose what they do with their leisure but there are some constraints in the society in which you live, such as government laws, social norms, conditioning, education and so on.
▶ Leisure activities have become important in society today because there is an increased demand by people who have more leisure time available for a greater variety of leisure activities. This has encouraged business organisations to supply an increasing variety of activities which cater for a whole spectrum of different people.

2 The role of leisure in society (past and present)

Aims

▶ To outline briefly leisure in pre-industrial societies
▶ To explain the role played by the industrial revolution in shaping today's society and leisure
▶ To describe and illustrate the 'work ethos' and its relationship to leisure activities
▶ To relate historical, economic and social factors to leisure
▶ To describe the influences that affect leisure today

Leisure in pre-industrial societies

Pre-industrial society describes a society in the stage before (or 'pre') large-scale development of manufacturing industry. In order to illustrate the different types of pre-industrial societies we have split them into two main types. The way these operate has a great effect on the people that live in them and their way of approaching 'leisure'. These are:

● A primitive society
● An agricultural society.

The primitive society is based on people hunting and gathering food, often travelling over large distances to do so. The people who live in this way are often nomads; whole families and communities may travel throughout the seasons of the year to different areas in search of food, or only some of the members of the community go and hunt for food, returning to the homelands when they are successful. Examples of this behaviour are declining due to the influence of Western society worldwide, but some societies, such as remote tribes in Africa, still follow this lifestyle.

The agricultural society describes a community which is settled in an area and cultivates crops; planting, harvesting and storing produce so that the people can survive until the next year. Examples of these societies are found throughout Asia, Africa and South America.

In a nomadic (or itinerant) society leisure activities are different to those pursued in a more settled community where there are usually more fixed routines. In the former leisure activities are linked to hunting or food gathering, such as taking part in festivals celebrating the hunt or the kill, carving wood or bone, sewing animal skins and so on. In a more settled community people are able to pursue a greater range of activities because they are not constantly travelling, e.g. artwork, wall painting, ceramics, sculpture, etc.

In both types of society whole families – grandparents, aunts, uncles, cousins, brothers and sisters, (much more extended than our idea of the family with one or two parents and children), all join in special events which involve dancing, chanting and playing musical instruments. These events may well continue for days and often mark certain festivals, such as weddings and the birth of children.

The industrial revolution in the UK and its effect on leisure

A definition of an industrial revolution is the change from a primitive or agricultural society which is mainly self-sufficient, into a society which depends on mass production methods and demand for goods and services. Thereafter people have to work in paid employment in order to earn the means to buy the basic essentials in order to live.

In Britain the industrial revolution began at the end of the eighteenth century (1760s onward), following the agricultural revolution that had begun in the 1750s. Production and processing of goods became more mechanised and faster, and by the 1830s factories were being built, and the division of labour and specialisation (rather than craft skills) was being developed.

For the people the industrial revolution meant a different style of living and great social and economic changes. The population of villages declined as new farming methods meant that fewer people were needed on the land. People drifted into towns and cities in search of work and an income in order that they could support themselves and their families. Living conditions became cramped and insanitary. Traditional skills of working in the home, such as weaving and spinning, were superceded by mechanised production in buildings which later became the great Victorian factories. People had to work in more formalised settings and with regulated hours. The time spent at work earning a living dictated how much time was left over for leisure interests and pursuits.

The transition

This transition and movement to an industrial society had far-reaching effects on the people, their style of living and where they lived. Even today there are countries and societies in the world which are reaching the point of industrialisation (parts of India and Africa, Pacific Island communities and tribal people of the South American Rain Forests), usually due to the influence of the Western world. People in these societies have to adjust from a subsistence lifestyle, relying on their communities and land to supply their needs, to looking outside the community for paid work. With these wages the families must purchase their means of survival. In many cases whole communities of people are tempted away from rural areas to urban areas for the promises of a cash wage and a better lifestyle.

The conditions in post-industrial revolution towns often became intolerable by today's standards of hygiene. The urban areas became overcrowded, housing conditions were poor (there was no running water nor adequate drainage systems) and disease caused by these conditions was rife. By the early nineteenth century pressure was put on the government by many social reformers and philanthropists to improve living conditions, and by the end of the 1880s most urban areas were providing sewers, running water, public baths, public parks and open spaces. The concept of government responsibility for the health and quality of life of the people was born.

The post-industrial revolution and leisure

The Victorian age (1837–1901)

This age become the milestone by which our leisure interests were shaped. Throughout the era the quality of people's lives and their expectations continued to rise. The urban population had a vast choice of entertainment in the form of theatres, music hall, gin palaces, roller and ice-skating and so on.

Victorian public amenities, such as parks and baths, still exist today and although many of them have had to have considerable improvement they remind us of the great age of building.

Science and nature   The Victorian age was the age of great scientific discoveries and technical progress. The environment was to prove very absorbing, wildlife, nature, rock formation, birds, plants and flowers were all studied, drawn and commented on. *The Country Diary of an Edwardian Lady*, a diary illustrated with detailed drawings of flowers and birds and describing the seasons' effect on nature, was only one of hundreds of similar notebooks kept by people throughout this time. Charles Darwin's theory of evolution fundamentally changed the way people looked at the world and our place within it.

Sport   Competitive sport increased in popularity during the Victorian era and different sports became regulated by modern rules. Cricket, rugby, football, tennis, boxing and hockey became similar to the activities we know today. For instance, the boys who attended the public school at Rugby had their lawless game regulated in 1846 and thereafter the game of rugby persisted. Gambling, corruption and bribes had been rife in the game of cricket and this became regulated by mid-century. Hockey was an extremely rough game until the Hockey Association was formed in 1886. Golf and rowing were exclusive sports, 'no menial or manual workers' were allowed to partake. Golf had been introduced from Scotland where it had been the national game. The Olympic Games were resurrected in 1896, after a gap of over 2000 years, and received entries from 22 countries.

Travel   The Victorian era saw the establishment of the British Empire; people travelled to far away places to catalogue and describe them, and to trade. Foreign influences from India, Africa, Canada, Australia, New Zealand and other places around the globe added to the British knowledge of world culture. The great explorers, such as Livingstone in Africa, and Burke and Wills in Australia, led expeditions to find out more about these places. The thirst for knowledge and for travel was unquenchable. The introduction of Thomas Cook's tours of foreign countries opened up places to people who would have never ventured abroad. The first one was in 1863 to Switzerland, followed by America in 1866, the Middle East in 1868 and round the world in 1872. This was the start of the foreign holiday, which is now an important part of the leisure industry.

Transport   People's leisure pursuits changed and benefited from the new railway system and improvements in roads and communications. Construction of the railway network began in the 1830s, opening up the countryside and the coastal regions. The Victorian age became the age of the seaside holiday or day trip. The trend for this started with the nobility in the late Georgian era, but now the general population could afford to go and had the means of transport available to them. The bicycle was invented in the 1860s and by 1888 J. B. Dunlop had adapted it for general use, enabling people to take trips into the countryside surrounding the towns. Eventually the motor car (1885) heralded the dawning of a new age; transport became less rigidly controlled by a timetable.

ACTIVITY

Read the article 'Oh, I do like to be beside the seaside', on page 14, and answer the following questions:

1   What were the reasons (according to the author of the article) for the development of the seaside holiday?

2   What economic implications did this have for the population and business organisations?

3   What kind of leisure pursuits do you think were popular on seaside holidays?

Oh, I do like to be beside the seaside!

by Edmund Swinglehurst

Ever since the British started taking holidays by the sea – effectively, from the mid-nineteenth century – life has been full of high expectations. At first it was the sheer wonder of it all that made any adventure seem possible. Was there really a mermaid in the striped tent on the beach fairground? Was that strange shape out at sea a serpent? Would the young man in a blazer and boater open up a conversation?

For people who had never seen the sea an unimaginably wider world was opening up, and the railways snaking out from the industrial towns became the pathways to a land of promise filled with sea water and shrimp teas. At first, a nation unused to unbridled pleasure – it was after all the Victorian age – was shy of letting its hair down and pulling its skirts up. But there were soon respected voices making reassuring noises. One of these was that of Dr Richard Granville who revived the idea of Dr Richard Russell, some decades earlier, that sea water was good for the health. To a nation already persuaded that minerals in water were salutary, it was not difficult to swallow the idea that salt, a mineral, must also be good for you. And swallow it they did, mixed with port or milk, according to taste, and, later, neat, and inadvertently, as the nation plunged into the sea.

Armed with a good excuse and provided for by railway transport which entrepreneurs were developing towards every bit of available coast, the masses began their annual pilgrimage to the briny. At first there were day trips, like the one organised by Thomas Cook in 1848 from Leicester to Scarborough, departing at midnight. Soon, however, property developers began to build houses which the better-off could rent or buy for the summer season. Many of these became boarding houses where guests provided their own food which was cooked, often villainously, by the landlady. The early seaside was, it seems, a chaotic place. The crowds pouring out of the excursion trains sometimes never reached the beach but spent the day in bars near the station. For those who did get there, the beach was a free-for-all, with couples hugging each other openly on the sands, musicians and entertainers creating a tumult, which led Charles Dickens to complain at Broadstairs that he could not get on with his work, with everyone having a good time. 'Everyone' included all the social classes of Britain, for the vastness of the seaside could accommodate everyone, unlike the cosy spas where everyone knew who everyone else was and was highly critical of anyone who did not fit in with spa society.

Extract from *The National Trust Magazine*,
No. 59, Spring 1990

Entertainment   The late nineteenth century heralded the introduction of the music hall show with singalongs, acting, cabaret and dancing. The wind-up gramophone played early musical recordings. It was not everyone's ideal, though. Many religious people found this type of behaviour quite scandalous and were much more content with passive pastimes of reading, embroidery, writing diaries and other such home-based activities.

Social class   The concept of working class, middle class and upper class were formalised in Victorian times. A person's class was dictated by a variety of different influences. In the main it was who a person's parents were, their income, wealth, money, education, social contacts, style of living, accent and so on which indicated their class in society. Class indicated all aspects of life, what work a person was expected to do, how one regarded others, where one lived and most importantly who one socialised with. Its importance to leisure cannot be understated because many leisure interests and activities could only apply to people of a certain status. Indeed many people would only be able to enjoy certain interests, for instance, cultural pursuits of the educated middle classes would have little interest to many working class people. Some sports, such as polo and hunting and entertainments like banqueting and dinner parties, could only be pursued by the upper classes who had the relevant social contacts. Many spontaneous and risqué entertainments like drinking, bare fist fighting, gambling and dog fighting would hold little enjoyment and may have been viewed with horror by the middle and upper classes.

If you have read any of Charles Dickens' novels (or have seen them serialised on TV), you will have some idea of the extent of the divided society in which the Victorians lived. This was also the age of the great philanthropists who studied and worked amongst people of all social classes and wrote about their lifestyles and interests. By studying these works we can form a clear image of their lives and leisure pursuits.

ACTIVITY

Discuss the following points with members of your group.

1 Why would some form of 'entertainments' have little appeal to other classes in society?

2 Was the lifestyle the majority of people lived directly linked to the types and variety of leisure activities they pursued?

3 Do you think that for the majority of the population their leisure activities were just forms of escapism from the life they led? If so, why?

The Victorian work ethos

In Victorian times, the work ethic was based on religious philosophy; if one excelled at work in this life, the rewards for one's labour would certainly be given in life after death. This rather morbid theory meant that wage rates did not have to be high and everyone was expected to work as many hours as possible. There was little time available for sports, leisure activities and pleasurable entertainments, and these were frowned upon if they detracted from 'work'. People were often expected to work six days a week for 17 hours a day, and on the seventh day (Sunday) they were expected to spend the day in religious activity (prayer and church going). Light entertainment was restricted to passive leisure activities, such as reading.

As you can imagine, during the working week there would be little time (or energy) to pursue leisure activities, and a person working in a factory, or 'in service' (i.e. a live-in servant), would be subject to restrictions such as brief formal meal and break times. Concentration was required for long time periods and people did not consider they were entitled to 'free time' (a concept we would find very strange today!).

In the 1870s the 60-hour working week became standard in the business environment. This was a time of falling prices, declining exports and a lowering of the rate of growth of industrial production, due to serious challenge from other newly industrialised nations.

The Cadbury factory in Birmingham was one of the pioneers in introducing a half-day holiday per week on a Saturday afternoon. By the end of the 1870s this had become the norm. On Sundays work was suspended due to religious observance and by the late 1870s the term 'weekend' was in common use. Bank holidays were also introduced around this time and some employers even allowed their workers one week's summer holiday (but this was often unpaid).

Leisure in the twentieth century

The First World War (1914–18)

War often emphasises the great contrasts in human behaviour; violence and hatred, and comradeship and love are concentrated in wartime. Great importance is placed upon socialising, entertainment and enjoyment. Lively entertainment like dancing, funfairs and parties are popular and passive pastimes like writing letters and diaries are also a very important leisure time pursuit.

The Sunshine Era

After the First World War people settled down to amusements such as holidaying on the coast. Sports such as playing tennis, croquet and swimming epitomised the Sunshine Era of the 1920s when there was a preoccupation with health and fitness and the great outdoors. 'Constitutionals' – long brisk walks – were recommended to prolong life and outdoor physical exercises (the weather was exceptionally good in the 1920s and 1930s), stretching, bending and generally loosening up were the norm. This was the age of Rag Time dances, shorter dresses, beads and clôche hats.

The preoccupation with the great outdoors was clearly demonstrated with the growth of the Boy Scout and Girl Guide movements in the 1920s. The Boy Scout movement was started by Robert Baden-Powell after 1908, and the Girl Guide movement was formed in 1910.

Other sports and fitness

Throughout the first half of the twentieth century motor racing, scrambling and touring gained popularity. The Isle of Man Tourist Trophy (TT) Race was established in 1907. As a means of transport the motorbike was relatively cheap and efficient; it enabled users to commute easily between villages and towns.

By 1934 National Playing Fields were established and games were allowed to be played in parks. In 1937 the government founded the National Fitness Council which gave £2 million in sports grants to voluntary bodies. There was a preoccupation with the idea that we were a C3 nation (that is one which is below par – unfit – or not A1). This had repercussions for the army as the majority of the population was not fit enough for active service, hence the government's idea that it should raise the health and fitness level of the nation.

Employment and leisure

During the 1920s and 1930s the working day became more structured, although work itself became increasingly hard to get. Unemployment in the mid-1920s to the mid-1930s meant more leisure time, which was often spent queuing for casual work. If you were 'in work' your standard of living gradually increased and you might be tempted to join in one of the cycle tour clubs or save to buy a motor car for trips to the countryside or the coast. Increasing popularity of motorised transport meant that a 30 mile-an-hour speed limit was imposed from 1934 onwards!

The Second World War (1939–45)

During the years 1939 to 1941 leisure pursuits followed the same trends as in the First World War. It was not until the United States of America joined forces with Britain in 1942 that spice was added to the social and entertainment scene of the wartime. New friendships, dances, bands and parties became part of the social scene at home.

The cinema, which had gained popularity in the 1920s, played soundtrack films from 1928 onwards and became one of the means by which the population was kept informed of news from abroad. Every household was equipped with a radio in order that they might be kept informed of the progress of the war, and it was by radio broadcast that Churchill made many of his famous speeches, designed to keep up morale. By the end of the war in 1946 a new social scene had emerged, to become known as youth culture.

Scouting for girls angers Guide chief

by Andrew Culf

The scouting movement is inviting girls up to 15 to join them around their camp fires as fully-fledged Scouts for the first time in 83 years.

They will join in the cooking and sing-songs but there will be separate tents and washing facilities.

Both the Scouts' Association and the Girl Guides Association were founded by Lord Baden-Powell and share the motto 'Be prepared' – but the announcement took the Guides by surprise.

Chief Commissioner Dr June Paterson-Brown said: 'I am extremely disappointed and cannot understand why they made this decision.' The two movements had discussed closer co-operation for two years, but the Scouts had unilaterally jumped the gun.

'I hope we are big enough to say that if the Scouts want this, it is their decision.' Although some girls would join to find out what it was like, she did not think the Guides would be greatly affected – although it would become a different matter if the Scouts tried to poach the Guides.

'We have had our ups and downs in our relationship but I hope we will continue to co-operate in the future.'

The Guides, with a membership of 733 000 compared to the Scouts' 680 000, plans to remain a single-sex organisation. 'We have had some boys who have asked if they can join but we will not take them,' said Dr Paterson-Brown.

Mr Derek Twine, executive commissioner of the Scouts' Association, said: 'There is no suggestion of us poaching, or recruiting from elsewhere.' Some girls would be attracted by camping, canoeing, and hiking from an earlier age.

Chief Scout Garth Morrison, making the announcement, said: 'We have to adapt to meet the needs of today's young people.

'We fully support the concept of single-sex youth work but, after a long hard look, we are convinced the opportunities provided by scouting should be available to all.

'We are aware that in some places there is a pressing need for it and we are anxious to meet that need. It is a move in the right direction.'

Local groups will decide whether or not to admit girls, and the Scouts insist there will be no pressure to conform.

Girls were first allowed to join in 1976 but only as Venture Scouts, a section which caters for 15 to 20-year-olds. There are 11 000 Venture Scouts, and mixed scouting exists in 50 countries.

Ms Nicola Lowes, from Wark, Northumbria, aged 14, hopes to become a Girl Scout. 'It is a great idea,' she said. 'I was in the Guides for a little while but I thought it was really boring.

'Scouts seem more active and you get outdoors more.'

Extract from *The Guardian*, 9 February 1990

ACTIVITY

Read the article and answer the following questions:

1 Why do you think it was necessary to form the separate movements of Scouts and Guides?

2 Why do you think the Guides wish to remain a single sex organisation?

3 Interview a member of the Scouts or Guides to find out what they think about the change that has occurred.

During the Second World War a longer working day was imposed on the home based population; 50 hours per week was standard in 1939 and plenty of overtime was available. Full employment meant that everyone had money to spend, but war time rationing meant there was little to spend it on (apart from the 'black market' goods sold under the counter!).

Leisure in the 1950s

This decade was marked with the growing importance of youth and their social scene. The 1950s saw the emergence of Teddy Boys; slicked-back hair and blue suede shoes. Listening and dancing to rock and roll music was the 'in' thing to do. Television was introduced in the home environment and this and the radio formed the basis of home entertainment. Leisure pursuits popular in this age included motor cycle scrambling, dog racing, all forms of gambling, watching and playing football. There was much diversity in the pursuits available and the availability of money to do them.

A post-war boom, in which Britain's trade thrived, meant a greater number of jobs available and therefore greater spending power in the form of wages or salaries. This money could be spent buying a new home (this period marked the increase in the number of owner-occupiers), so therefore decorating, making furnishings and DIY were added to the lists of hobbies and pastimes. Labour-saving devices such as washing machines, vacuum cleaners and electric irons became necessary in every home. For women this meant a reduction in the time spent on household chores and for many people an increase in time to spend in other ways.

Leisure in the 1960s

The trends of the 1950s continued into the early 1960s. By the late 1960s the hippy movement advocated peace and love and passive leisure pursuits like sitting contemplating the universe, yoga, and smoking. Travel also featured; the young 'discovered' India and the Asian continent, Australia, New Zealand, America and the meaning of life. The older generation took the new-fangled 'package' tour to Spain as an alternative to holidaying in England, Wales and Scotland. Mods and rockers invaded seaside resorts in the summertime. Their leisure time pursuits were also passive, riding motorbikes, listening to music, drinking alcohol and looking menacing were part of their culture.

▶
The flower power era; youth culture of the 1960s

Leisure in the 1970s

In the 1970s the economic affluence began to fade a little. Youth culture changed to the skinheads (who had been around since the late 1960s) and punks with outlandish hairstyles and clothes. Both groups had their own ideas about music and dancing and escapist pursuits; drinking and drugtaking were actively undertaken by many.

Holidays and travel were still important and package tour holiday destinations became further afield. Television and video watching dominated some people's lives. Collectors of various paraphernalia – antiques, books, dolls, bottles, etc. – scouted round to increase their collections as a hobby.

Political influence in sport started to occur in the 1950s. The Russians spent a vast amount of money on athletes in order to almost ensure success in competition sport. The apartheid policies of South Africa meant that many people refused to play sport there. The Israel and Arabic conflict and ensuing terrorist violence affected the sporting world.

Leisure in the 1980s

Although the 1980s was marked by an increase in unemployment, by contrast some of the employed enjoyed far more disposable income than ever before. (Disposable income is the money you have in your pocket for spending after all statutory deductions, e.g. National Insurance and tax, have been paid.) The growth of commercial leisure centres, which linked sport to socialising, is an important feature of this age, and leisure itself took on a greater significance due to a shorter working week and a greater number of people having more time to take up leisure interests.

Since the Victorian age the concept of class has declined in importance and most leisure pursuits have become open to all. However, there are still expensive leisure pursuits; yachting, three-day eventing, ballooning, flying, and status-orientated leisure activities such as polo, are largely followed by small groups of wealthy people or those who have the social contacts necessary to pursue these activities.

ACTIVITY

1 From this chapter choose the era in history that most interests you. Use the research facilities available in your local library to find out more about the leisure pursuits of the era you have chosen (remember that leisure activities are not just sports!).

2 Write down the information that you find in note form, being careful to include details of the source of the information (that is the author's name, name of publication, date of publication, publisher).

3 Use the notes you have collected on your chosen subject to write a report, giving an account of the leisure activities of that time. Attach a bibliography to the report which gives the details of the sources you have used.

The current influences on leisure

We have inherited traditions, attitudes and knowledge from other periods in time and have a greater choice of leisure time pursuits than ever before. Five major areas that influence the way people perform and enjoy leisure activities are illustrated in Figure 2.1, page 20, and explained below:

1 The society you live in
2 The environment
3 Professional and commercial life
4 Home and personal life
5 Recreational amenities.

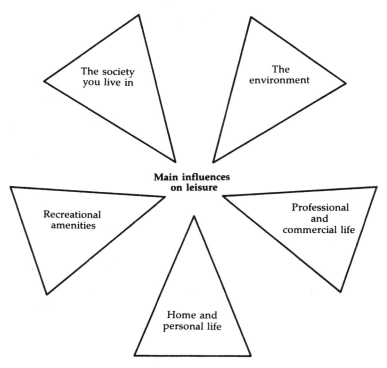

▲ *Figure 2.1   Main influences on leisure*

1 The society you live in

One of the most important influences on a person's leisure pursuits must be the social and economic environment in which they live. This can include:

- *Standard of living*   How 'well off' a person is, in material terms: for instance, whether they have the most up-to-date consumer goods in their home and can afford expensive leisure pursuits.

- *Politics*   Which political party governs the country and how much of the resources are allocated to leisure amenities.

- *Religion*   A person's religion may have some bearing on the leisure activities undertaken and the time devoted to these interests.

- *Laws*   Laws can ban some activities and help to promote others, e.g. the banning of cruel sports.

- *The history of society*   Which traditions are continued in sports, entertainment and pastimes.

- *Physical location in the world*   Where a person lives often dictates what type of leisure activities are pursued; for instance, in the Northern or Southern hemisphere, whether a developed or an undeveloped nation, in the west or east, north or south.

- *Availability of education services*   Teachers, trainers, and resources like books and equipment are necessary so that people can pursue cultural and educational leisure pursuits.

- *International influences*   Trading partners throughout the world affect the leisure activities and sports in your country.

- *Nationalistic pride*   How a nation views itself and whether the population is very patriotic and has a national sport.

- *Matriarchal or patriarchal societies*   Whether it is the mother or the father who has the last say in what goes on in the family home life affects the kind of leisure activities the family is allowed to take part in.

- *Social class or status*   In many societies there is a hierarchy of social order and it can be very difficult to converse with and relate to other people who are not of the same social standing. This affects the leisure pursuits each group gets involved in.

- *Autocracy or democracy*   This is linked to the system of government that a country has. Within a democracy the people vote in the government and therefore have a greater say in what goes on within the country. In an autocracy the people are told what to do; if the autocratic government dictates that the people can only pursue their leisure activities on certain days then this has to be so.

- *Monarchy*   Not every country has a royal family, but often if a royal family member patronises a certain sport or activity this becomes very popular.

- *Technology available*   If a country is one of the world leaders in technical progress, this will have a spin-off effect on leisure in two ways. Firstly it will affect the time people have to spend in paid employment and hence their leisure time and secondly more technical progress will affect the type of leisure activities (e.g. video games, hi-tech amusement arcades).

- *Population statistics*   Often a nation with an increasing population has less money income per head available to develop sports and leisure facilities. Most of the income is diverted to keep people fed and clothed. With a low rate of population growth the society can afford to enhance standards of living and quality of life and hence leisure becomes more important.

- *People's attitudes*   These depend on what is regarded as 'normal' or the 'norm' in the society that you live in. If sport and leisure are encouraged, then people are encouraged to be involved in these activities.

You can see from the above that the society in which you live has a direct influence on the leisure activities that take place – however, there are also other categories to consider.

2 Environmental factors

The physical surroundings of the area in which you live – either the natural features or the man-made facilities and amenities that the area offers – have an important influence on leisure. For example, people who live near the sea are more likely to go sailing than people who live inland. The list below gives a broad idea of the most important environmental factors:

- Raw materials or resources (such as minerals)
- Soil type (chalk/sand/clay, etc.)
- Climate or weather conditions
- Landscape (flat or mountainous).
- Plants
- Woodland
- Animals
- Birds

ACTIVITY

You may like to consider your own area.

1 Work through the list above and jot down the environmental features that it has – for example, the type of climate, soil, landscape, etc.

2 How do these affect the leisure pursuits available? (For example, if you live in a mountainous region then it will be likely that you can go rock climbing, hill walking, caving, etc. If you live by inland waterways you might be able to go sailing, waterski-ing, etc.)

3 Professional and commercial life

In all developed societies there is an environment for economic activity to take place, e.g. trading, buying and selling. This generates three types of income:

- For the businesses themselves (profits)
- For the workers and their families (wages)
- For the government (taxation).

The amount of commercial activity and income generated in a country influences the amount and type of leisure activities that take place. The more income there is to spare in a society the more incentive there is for businesses to provide commercial facilities and thereby to generate profit.

ACTIVITY

1 Conduct a mini-survey of your friends and acquaintances. Do they take days off from paid employment as a result of illness caused by their leisure pursuits?

2 How fit would you regard these people?

3 Suggest ways to rectify the problem of absence through illness caused by leisure activities.

---

4 Home, personal life and character

This covers the more personal details of your life and what influences you as an individual. Your need to undertake leisure activities or sports depends on the following:

- Your image and the clothing you wear
- Your normal behaviour patterns
- Time taken to undertake essential activities and household chores
- Relaxing time available
- Disposable income
- Peer group pressure
- Competitive behaviour
- Age
- Sex
- Health
- Education
- Mood
- Personality.

For example, a young fashion-conscious student with a bright and lively personality would be far more likely to pursue physically demanding and popular sports such as mountain cycling and roller or ice skating. A retired person with a quieter attitude to life might enjoy walking and going to the theatre.

5 Recreational amenities

The greater the number of leisure facilities or amenities that are provided the 'richer' the society will be in terms of leisure provision. The choice for the average user will be greater.

These points should be considered:

- Availability of organised facilities/amenities
- Cost/price of these
- Government assistance/provision of amenities

- Necessity and availability of special clothing and equipment
- Time necessary to learn activities
- Whether there are trained staff supervising and teaching users.

The role of leisure in society

We have seen in this chapter how important leisure as a concept is in the society we live in. The work ethos of paid employment in a formal environment defined how much more time people could spend on other activities. The decline of opportunities for paid employment, unemployment and other forms of 'work' influences peoples' approach to leisure in modern society.

Leisure is important because:

1 It enhances the quality of life in society.
2 It relaxes, stimulates, may promote health and fitness and can be fun.
3 It can be educational and cultural.
4 It can make use of 'spare time' that may otherwise have been wasted, i.e. 'constructive use' of leisure time.
5 Leisure activities and sports can be encouraged and may prevent anti-social acts, such as crime.
6 Leisure involves commercial activity and so generates demand for goods and services which in turn generates income and employment.
7 It allows people in society to develop a wide variety of skills.
8 It allows for healthy competition between both individuals and businesses.
9 It is a focus for tradition and history in society and skills handed down in families.

Summary

▶ In pre-industrial societies the concept of leisure or recreation is very different to that of developed societies because the pace of life is generally slower and there are fewer structured routines. Group entertainment, for example, festive occasions such as weddings and carnivals, are typical recreational activities enjoyed by members of these societies.
▶ Since the Industrial Revolution patterns of work have meant that times for leisure recreation are more strictly defined. Leisure time is often regarded as the time to rest between work periods. Attitudes to leisure encourage this as a pleasurable activity in contrast to humdrum working life.
▶ Historical factors (e.g. laws, society, economic progress, social and political change) have shaped the types and forms of leisure, entertainment, sport and recreation that we pursue today.
▶ The development of commerce has had a great impact on leisure; on the one hand it provides a greater scope for different types of recreation and entertainment and on the other it provides work and has therefore created a greater number of jobs and income.
▶ Sports have been developing into the form that we know them since the nineteenth century. There are governing bodies or associations who have laid down clearly defined sets of rules. This has assisted both amateur and professional players.
▶ Current influences on leisure are numerous and continue to develop and shape a person's use of leisure and the way society as a whole views recreational activities.

A DISPLAY

Complete in-depth research into the leisure activities of the past 100 years and produce a display. The themes for your leisure display are set out below; choose one theme per group.

1 **Transport, sport and pastimes** – the effect that the technical revolution in transport and communications has had on sport, leisure and pastimes.
2 **The demise of the working day** – the effect unemployment and the shorter working week has had on leisure and sports.
3 **National security and leisure** – the effect that the two World Wars have had on sport, leisure and entertainment.
4 **Education and leisure** – the impact on state schooling and the education system on sports and recreation.
5 **Entertainment and change** – changes in the commercial providers of entertainment in your area.
6 **Growth and change of the seaside holiday** – how the location and preference for certain holiday destinations has changed.

Use as many source materials as possible; the following are some suggestions:

● Interviews with the older generation to find out what they remember.
● Photographs, memorabilia from your relatives and friends.
● Books, magazines, and newspaper articles from the local history section of your local library (the local history section usually has old photographs that the staff will let you look at and perhaps copy).
● Current articles from TV programmes, radio programmes, local newspapers (most local newspaper offices have a library section you might use to help you locate journalists' articles on local history).

Once you have collected all your material, arrange it into a display or exhibition which could be accommodated in your local library, community centre, school, or college. Remember to include text so that the subject is fully understandable, and make the display as eye-catching as possible. You may be surprised how interested members of the general public are in these topics. One of the problems you will need to overcome (or one of the skills you need to acquire) is how to deal with people who will not stop reminiscing!

The provision of leisure facilities for communities

Aims

▶ To underline the diversity of the leisure industry
▶ To assess the provision for leisure in your area
▶ To introduce the concept of user groups
▶ To understand the difference between natural resources and built facilities
▶ To outline the difference between leisure centres and leisure facilities

Leisure resources

Look around the area in which you live and consider the range of leisure facilities provided for the community. What about the park you used to play in as a child or the youth club in the community centre you may now attend? Do you live near the sea or is there a lake or reservoir near you, where people participate in water sports? Are there 'natural' leisure resources, such as hills or mountains where people can walk and climb or even ride mountain bikes? Does the local school/college offer evening classes? What range of leisure facilities/activities does it offer?

By examining the range of resources and facilities contributing to the leisure industry in your own locality you will soon realise how diverse the leisure industry is. There is a wide variety of private, public and voluntary organisations which serve the needs of the local community.

There are two main types of leisure resources; **natural**, e.g. the sea, lakes, rivers or mountains, or **built**, e.g. a zoo, theatre or sports hall.

The difference between a **leisure facility** and a **leisure centre** is that the facility is an amenity which assists the process of 'leisure' (a park, or gravel pits); a leisure centre is far more specific as it refers to a purpose-built indoor or outdoor amenity, such as a sports hall or a theme park.

Natural resources

Some areas have the advantage of natural resources such as the sea, mountains, lakes, rivers, forests and so on. However, although the resources already exist, they often have to be managed and planned in order to ensure that they are safe and pleasant facilities for users.

Water resources

The sea, lakes and rivers need to be protected from pollution to make them safe for water sports enthusiasts, sailing clubs, canoeing clubs and anglers. This enables people to use the facilities safely, in the company of others. The lifeboat sea rescue service is an added safety factor which can be called upon as a last resort. However, some sports or activities directly conflict with others. For instance, fishing does not co-exist well with water ski-ing, and so there has to be a clear management plan for different water amenities, providing clear guidelines as to who can use the facility at what time and for what purpose. Some parts of the amenity may be reserved only for certain types of activities, e.g. windsurfing and canoeing.

Durdle Door, Dorset. Natural resources can
be used for leisure purposes

Hills and mountains

As more people are using these areas for walking and climbing they need to be conserved through organisations such as the Countryside Commission and National Parks Authorities. Mountain biking is also an increasingly popular leisure activity.

The Mountain Rescue Service provides a measure of safety for the more adventurous who find themselves in difficulty in the mountains.

ACTIVITY

Refer to the index of leisure activities in Appendix 1 (page 164).

1 Work through the list alphabetically and note down at least 10 activities that need a mountainous or hilly landscape.

2 Decide which of these activities are compatible, i.e. can be performed without conflicting with other users performing different leisure and sports activities. Make a list of those that are incompatible.

3 How might you solve the problems you have outlined in Task **2** (above)? Discuss these issues with the group.

Built facilities

Built facilities are 'man-made' and may be indoor or outdoor. Sometimes they have been built specifically for the purpose of leisure (e.g. a leisure centre) or sometimes leisure is a secondary activity, such as a stately home where there is a resident landlord/lady, or a water reservoir which is primarily used to provide water but is also used for water sports.

Some of the facilities may have been originally built for other purposes and have been converted into leisure facilities. Modern purpose-built facilities usually cater for the needs of disabled users (e.g. disabled lifts, ramps and toilets, see Chapter 9).

▲ *Old buildings in urban areas have been used for many purposes, e.g. a purpose-built cinema is used as a bingo hall*

In order to understand the diverse nature of leisure facilities it is useful to build up a leisure map of your local area. Figure 3.1 illustrates a town centre and shows the variety of sports, social, entertainment and leisure places available in this urban area. You will see that any leisure facility that you study has a varied and interesting history and depends on the continued interest of its users in order to survive.

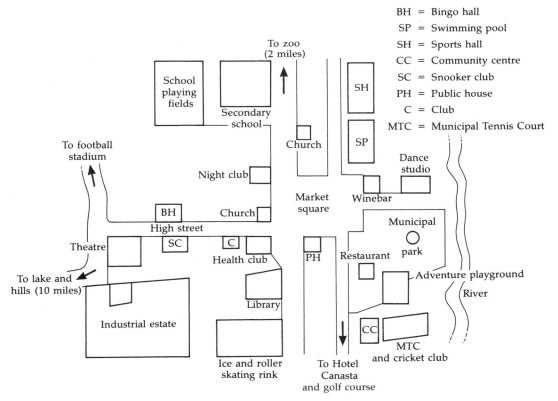

▲ *Figure 3.1   South Harding Leisure Map*

South Harding leisure facilities

You will appreciate that many of the facilities available in your locality have existed for many years. Let us look more closely at the background of leisure facilities in South Harding. The football club is in the Third Division of the Football League and there are plans to refurbish the ground in an effort to attract a wider range of supporters, particularly families.

Bingo, a game particularly enjoyed by women in the town, is on offer every afternoon and evening. The town's cricket team might enjoy a post-game drink in the pub, which is owned and run by a major brewery.

The Hotel Canasta (four star) is newly built and caters for visiting business people, who have full use of the hotel's leisure club.

The younger members of the community meet at the roller/ice skating rink, where disco evenings are popular.

On Sundays, after the religious service at the church, some people walk their dogs in the park while children enjoy themselves in the adventure playground provided by the local council.

The theatre was built in 1880 and has been open ever since, even though a fire threatened to close it in the Second World War blitz of 1943.

The swimming pool opened in 1963 and is owned by the local authority. It was designed for lane swimming, but there are now plans to develop a leisure pool with a water slide and wave machine to cater for 'fun' swimming.

The secondary school has its own playing field but has joint use of the sports hall, which is used by the community in the evenings. The sports hall was built in 1985 with funds provided jointly by the Sports Council and the Local Authority. The school rents out its pitches to local clubs. In the evening the school operates a variety of evening classes.

The snooker club operates from an old cinema, which was renovated in the late 1970s. It operates on a membership only scheme and has a bar and two pool tables.

The local community centre was provided by the local authority and a community development officer has been appointed to run the facility and to encourage use by all types of local people.

The private health club is exclusive and offers tailor-made fitness programmes for members. It has a solarium, two saunas, a whirlpool and two squash courts. It has been open for 18 months and is located on the industrial estate.

For those who like the outdoors, canoeing or rowing, the river is a possibility. Alternatively, windsurfing and sailing on the lake (which is owned by the Water Authority) is an all year-round possibility for the hardier members of the community.

The mountaineering club benefits from the position of the local crags and hills.

ACTIVITY

1 Look at the list of user groups opposite. From the map in Figure 3.1 draw up a list of the facilities that each group is likely to use.

2 In Chapter 1 you learnt that a person with paid employment will probably only be able to use leisure facilities or centres during lunchtimes or evenings. In contrast a person who is unemployed, works shifts or works at home may well be free during daytime hours and would welcome the opportunity to use facilities outside 'peak' times.

  Using the map in Figure 3.1 and the text for reference indicate the type of activity that you would expect to be offered to each group by the organisations/facilities in South Harding, and when they would be likely to use the facilities.

User groups	Facilities	Activities	Main leisure time
• Senior citizens	Bingo Hall Community Centre	Bingo/Bowls	Day/off-peak

- Young working males
  16 to 29 age group
- Young working females
  16 to 29 age group
- School age children
- A parent at home with
  children under five
  years old
- Disabled people
- Business men/women
  30 years and over
- Unemployed people
- Ethnic minorities

Tourism

The growth of the tourism industry is linked with the growth in leisure facilities. When tourists visit areas they create a demand for goods, services and leisure activities.

The leisure activities are provided for tourists by either entrepreneurs or local authorities. Tourism may have a seasonal effect on local trade as it may be linked to the climate of an area and holiday periods, e.g. in Great Yarmouth in Norfolk the tourist is catered for by the businesses on the Golden Mile of seafront, but only during the 'summer season' (Easter to the end of September) when the weather is hopefully conducive to seaside activities. In the winter months the majority of businesses close down and the place becomes depopulated. There is seasonal unemployment and businesses have to ensure that they have made enough money in the summer months to ride out the winter downturn in trade.

However, patterns of tourist demand have changed in recent years, with many people showing an interest in more independent and adventurous holidays. Increasingly resorts have developed leisure facilities available for 'all year-round activities', e.g. timeshare developments in the Lake District, with swimming pools, saunas and jacuzzis, providing 'leisure centres' for the whole area. In ski resorts more efficient lift systems have been built, with some sites offering artificial snow if natural falls are insufficient. In the summer months the lifts are used by summer hikers, so ski resorts offer year-round facilities.

ACTIVITY

1 Do many tourists visit the area in which you live? If so, why? If not, why not?

2 Pinpoint the leisure facilities which are mainly geared to the tourist trade.

3 List other leisure facilities which you think would attract more tourists to your area. Give reasons.

Summary

▶ Leisure amenities can be categorised into natural and built facilities, both of which have to be managed in order to maximise use by the public.

▶ Local leisure facilities may be purpose built (e.g. a swimming pool) or may have developed as a secondary use for the facility (e.g. a castle which becomes a tourist attraction).

▶ Different user groups in an area demand different leisure activities. The time people have available for leisure activities varies and so their use of facilities also differs.

▶ The tourist industry may affect local provision of leisure facilities and therefore there may be a greater number of amenities available, although these could be subject to seasonal fluctuations.

Assignment 2

YOUR LOCAL LEISURE FACILITIES

Visit the Planning Department of the Town Hall and obtain a map which features the various city or town wards (this map may possibly be obtained from the local library or Tourist Information Bureau). If you live in a rural area look at an ordnance survey map and carry out your study in a three-mile radius of where you live.

Either work in a group or individually and choose one or more wards for the purposes of your investigation. If working in a group each member should be assigned certain roads and should undertake a survey of that area, marking all leisure facilities on a map.

Find out the following basic information about each facility identified:

- Ownership
- Range of activities
- Extent of facilities
- Opening hours
- Membership details
- Prices
- Publicity material
- Access for able-bodied and disabled users.

Produce a display for an event such as an open evening or a community centre display, using the information you have gathered.

4 / *The leisure providers*

Aims

▶ To introduce the concept of a mixed economy
▶ To introduce the provision of leisure facilities in the public sector
▶ To introduce the provision of leisure facilities in the private sector
▶ To introduce the provision of leisure facilities in the voluntary sector

Leisure provision in a mixed economy

There are three main categories of leisure providers:

- Government provision (public sector)
- Private provision (private sector)
- Voluntary provision (voluntary sector).

Public sector provision

The leisure industry reflects the mixed economy of the UK. The state (e.g. central or local government organisations) provides leisure activities and facilities in the **public sector**. In theory the public sector facilities exist to provide a service to the community (a service in this context means something that benefits or is useful to the members of the public in the area).

Private sector provision

Alternatively, the **private sector** of the leisure industry involves business organisations, owned by individuals or groups of people, which are not controlled by the state. Business organistions in this sector intend to operate for profit. This means that the money the businesses receive from trading (i.e. from selling their goods or services to customers or clients) must be more than is spent on buying stock or providing services.

Voluntary sector provision

Falling between the public sector and the private sector is the **voluntary sector**, which embraces all kinds of organisations, such as clubs, societies and charities. These are neither controlled by the state nor operated solely for profit. They have been formed because of some interest or need in the community.

The main sectors in the leisure industry

Public sector
For example:

- Municipal swimming pool
- Local authority sports centre
- Parks

Private sector

For example:

- Oasis Leisure Centre
- Rollaball bowling alley
- Alton Towers Theme Park

Voluntary sector

For example:

- Local youth club
- The Royal Society for the Protection of Birds
- Scouts, Guides, etc.

> ## ACTIVITY
>
> The ownership of various organisations is sometimes not immediately apparent. The list above gives a few examples of ownership. Look around your locality and categorise the various types of leisure facilities available to the community into public sector, private sector and voluntary sector ownership. Use the information you collect to draw up a list similar to the one above. You will build on this information in a later activity.
>
> You might have to ask a few questions to ascertain ownership of some facilities; if you are polite, employees and others will be only too willing to assist you.

Joint ventures

You may well discover some surprising facts when you start asking questions. A few organisations can be owned by the state (i.e. operating in the public sector), but some parts of them may be 'privatised' (i.e. in the private sector). For example, in a local authority leisure centre the restaurant and catering facilities may be serviced by a privately-owned firm which supplies its own staff and equipment. The cleaning operations may also be undertaken by a private firm. Alternatively a local authority and a private developer may develop a new swimming pool or sports complex as a joint venture.

▶ The Oasis Leisure Centre, Swindon: an example of a public sector leisure centre

Privatisation

Sometimes state-owned enterprises have been 'privatised' completely. This means they are taken out of state control (the public sector) and now operate in the private sector (see Chapter 5).

Voluntary sector organisations may also have to resort to commercial pressure in order to obtain funds. They become a 'commercial charity' which means that they are organised like a private sector business organisation and have sales and marketing and membership departments. Examples are the Royal Society for the Protection of Birds and the National Trust.

Legal forms of business

In the private sector there are different forms of business operation; e.g. sole traders, partnerships, private limited companies, public limited companies, and co-operatives. Further information is found in Chapter 7.

Private sector sports facility on Mull for public use

by Eric M Macintyre

Sporting booms occur much later in the Scottish Highlands and Islands than in more densely populated areas, but when they do they tend to be more dramatic than normal. For example on the Isle of Mull the game of squash is currently in vogue with the islanders, at the same time adding a new twist to the public *v.* private debate on leisure facility provision.

The story began when Major Raymond Nelson, a former member of the British Army squash team, took over the Glengorm Estate near Tobermory in 1968, with its working farm and nineteenth century castle. No facilities existed on Mull for squash and the Major long cherished an ambition to build a court for his own and public use. He finally got round to seriously considering the matter in the last couple of years and his chosen venue was a 200-year-old cattle byre. The chance availability of a second-hand court in Dorset was the real trigger for the project and undaunted by the distance for transportation the Major bought it. He then did much of the conversion work himself along with Tobermory joiner

Angus Robertson. Luxurious changing rooms and showers were added, and the court was officially opened by Mrs Ray Michie, Argyll's MP, last September.

And although Major Nelson put up £40 000 for the court himself, he always intended it for public use. The local school has now taken out a block membership and a club has been formed with over 100 members. A local sports shop, Togs and Clogs, handles the bookings in return for racquet hire and sales and sponsorship has also been found, with the Clydesdale Bank donating the club's first trophy.

Raymond Nelson hopes to re-coup some of his outlay through grants from the Highlands and Islands Development Board or other agencies like the Scottish Sports Council. Until then he must content himself with having created a sudden rise in popularity of a game previously unknown on the Isle of Mull. As for the players, they are consoled by the thought that if exhaustion takes over, there are stout 200-year-old walls to lean against and a view that must be unrivalled by any other squash court in the world.

Article from *Sports and Leisure,*
January/February 1986

Read the article 'Private sector sports facility on Mull for public use' and the notes below.

Notes

Major Nelson has put up personal funds to invest in the scheme, yet if he is able to re-coup some of the money from the Highlands and Islands Development Board the scheme will become more than just a private sector scheme. It will be an example of joint provision between a private developer (Major Nelson) and the public sector (the Development Board being part of the state). The scheme itself is not just profit-orientated but aims to provide an amenity for the islanders and will hopefully promote health and fitness for the users.

Answer the following questions:

1 Who gains from the introduction of this facility on the island?

2 What problems can you envisage at the court?

3 How can these be overcome?

4 Why would the Highlands and Islands Development Board invest money or give a grant to the scheme?

5 Why do you think Major Nelson introduced the facility?

◾ Aims and objectives of leisure providers

The aims and objectives of the various organisations involved in the leisure industry can vary considerably. The aims are distinct from the objectives, in that they are broad concepts which the organisation seeks to attain; in other words, the purpose for which an organisation exists. The objectives are more specific and can be described as something at which an organisation directs itself. Objectives are sometimes referred to as specific goals or destinations.

In any business organisation the aims and objectives depend on which sector (e.g. public, private or voluntary) the organisation operates in.

Aims of leisure organisations

Public sector

The aims of a leisure organisation in the public sector (e.g. a municipal swimming pool) might be:

- To provide a service for the population in the surrounding area, perhaps in order to improve health and fitness in that area, or to improve social amenities.
- To keep within the local authority budget and to make an adequate return on the local authority capital invested in the organisation.
- To provide jobs for people in the locality.

These aims are influenced by:

- Politics: for example changes of government – a Conservative government would tend to reduce spending in the public sector, whereas a Labour government would tend to increase spending where there was more social need for services.
- The money and resources available in a country – known as the economic climate; a country with a population that has a high standard of living and a high rate of economic growth can afford to spend more on leisure services.

- The society as a whole – for example, what the people expect the state to provide. People in different countries throughout the world have different expectations of state involvement in the economy.

Many local authority organisations have leisure aims laid down by statute (i.e. law) and there may well be a legal obligation on the authority to provide certain services such as museums, libraries and education. These obligations are imposed by central government.

Private sector

The aims of leisure organisations in the private sector may vary considerably depending on the legal form they take (e.g. sole trader, partnership, private limited company and so on). For example:

- Profit maximisation may be an overriding priority for some organisations: in a limited company the shareholders may only hold shares in that company if they get an adequate return. If profits and dividends fall they will sell their shares which could lead to problems for the company (see Chapter 7). Survival may also be a distinct aim, e.g. to survive a downturn in trade in the hope of a better future in the next few years.
- A private club, on the other hand, may aim to cater for the needs of its members in a particular sporting activity, e.g. snooker.
- More aggressive private sector organisations may aim to increase their market share (see Chapter 13) in direct competition with similar business organisations offering products or services. For example, a sports shop may aim to progress from a local organisation based in one town to a regional or national company with many branches, by competing, taking over or merging with other companies selling similar products.

▶ *The Ritzy Nightclub, Swansea: an example of a private sector club providing late night entertainment*

- Some leisure or sporting organisations might aim to improve their public image – for example, a commercial sports centre using recycled paper products in order to be recognised as environmentally friendly.
- Another aim might be to maintain a constant cash flow, i.e. keeping money flowing into and out of the organisation, and not allowing debts to pile up.

Voluntary sector

The aims of leisure organisations in the voluntary sector could include the following broad issues:

- To provide facilities that are not provided either by the state or by a private sector organisation, e.g. a youth club in a village.
- To strictly observe a non-profit making rule, ensuring that any surplus income over expenditure that the organisation makes goes back to its members or is invested in the organisation's future. The National Trust operates in this way.
- To bring to the public's attention some problem in society, e.g. conservation issues or environmental protection. These organisations are known as pressure groups, and include, for example, Friends of the Earth and Greenpeace.
- There may be some political or social aim or reason for the organisation's existence – for example, to encourage 'constructive use' of leisure, such as the Scouts, or the Guides.

Objectives in the public sector

The objectives of a public sector organisation are more specific than those of the voluntary sector organisation. For example, in the public sector a local authority sports centre might have as an aim the promotion of fitness in the locality. It might take this one stage further to specifically promote one type of sport, such as football for the under-21s. Alternatively, an aim might be to create employment and an objective might be to create a certain number of jobs per year.

Objectives in the private sector

In the private sector the objective of a sports club might be to join a certain national league. A profit-orientated organisation might have as an objective the increasing of turnover by, say, 10 per cent per annum.

Objectives in the voluntary sector

In the voluntary sector an objective may be to recruit a certain number of members per year, or to hold a number of social functions in a month, or to raise a sum of money for a specific purpose. Raising money for the purchase of a recreation area or building for use by young people, within a certain time limit, may be the objective of a youth club.

ACTIVITY

From the information you gathered in the activity on page 32 pick one organisation from each sector on your list. Examine these organisations critically and decide the following:

1 Three aims of the organisations.

2 Three of the possible objectives of the organisations. It is probable that you will not be certain of these unless you contact the organisation directly.

3 Distinguish the aims and objectives of three more leisure organisations that are familiar to you.

Ownership and control of leisure organisations

The **owner** of a business organisation is the person, or group of people, legally responsible for its operation. The owner has invested the capital (or money) in the venture and stands to take the profits, or bear the losses if necessary.

The person or group of people **controlling** the organisation is responsible for its day-to-day operation and policy-making, but does not necessarily own the business, or have capital or money invested in it.

In many cases (such as very large business operations) it is possible to distinguish between the owners and the controllers of the business. For example, in a large company operating in the private sector (e.g. Mecca Leisure PLC) the owners are the shareholders who have invested capital in the venture and who may ultimately lose out if the business has to close, i.e. they will lose the money they have invested. Alternatively, if the business makes a profit they stand to gain financially, in the form of **dividends** on their shares. Depending on how well the company operates these shares may increase in value and can be sold for more than they were purchased for.

The controllers may be elected by the shareholders to be **directors** of the business. The managers and administration staff may be recruited by the Personnel Department of the company. Usually the directors deal with policy-making of the business venture and the managers deal with the day-to-day operations.

Sometimes the directors and managers are also shareholders and thus they become both owners and controllers. In these large companies ownership is fragmented because so many people own shares, so no one person has complete ownership. A public limited company might have several thousand shareholders. The control of the company is not vested in just one person but in a group of people (e.g. the board of directors) and the total workforce.

Alternatively in a small business, such as a sole trader, (e.g. Ben Smith's Sports Shop) just one person is vested with the ownership and the control of the business. The person who puts up the capital for the enterprise and takes the profit or bears the losses also organises the business rationale and controls the day-to-day affairs.

In the public sector the state owns the business organisations. It can be said that as the state is made up of members of the public, the ultimate owner of any state or public enterprise is the people of that country. The people elect a government to run state affairs for them and therefore place the control of the public enterprises in the hands of the government or local authority officials.

Summary

- ▶ There are three main sectors of the economy in the UK: private, public and voluntary.
- ▶ Often the boundaries between the sectors become blurred if there are joint ventures or privatisation occurs.
- ▶ All organisations have aims and objectives and these are formulated in order to give direction to an organisation.
- ▶ There can be a distinction between the owners of an organisation and the people who control the general activities of that organisation.
- ▶ It used to be assumed that private sector organisations only operated for a profit and public sector organisations only operated as a service to members of the public. The situation is now more complex due to stricter budgeting in the public sector and greater consumer awareness in the private sector.

5 The role of central government in leisure

Aims

▶ To identify which areas of the state affect the leisure environment
▶ To illustrate which central government departments are involved in leisure provision
▶ To show how law making affects the leisure industry
▶ To illustrate the effect of privatisation and compulsory competitive tendering on leisure provision in the public sector

State provision of leisure amenities

The state may have total control of planning and operating activities that occur in a country as, for example, in a centrally planned system such as China, where all amenities and leisure facilities are controlled by government, which decides what should be provided, how this should be done and who should be allowed to use the facilities. In other countries the opposite situation exists, where the state has a very low profile and all leisure facilities are provided by business organisations in the private sector (the free market economy). For example, in the USA the government provides little in the way of recreational amenities, but gives encouragement to other organisations to do this.

In the UK the state-provided leisure amenities in the public sector exist side by side with those in the private sector. In the public sector, the leisure amenities are provided by four different bodies:

1 Central government
2 Local government
3 Nationalised industries (also known as public corporations)
4 Regional authorities.

Central government

Central government is an integral part of the leisure and sporting environment in the UK. It affects the industry in the following ways:

● It has the power to create other organisations which in turn specialise in the provision of some aspect of the leisure industry, e.g. the Countryside Commission and English Heritage.
● It provides subsidies or grants to various organisations in order to assist the provision of leisure or sport facilities, e.g. the Sports Council and the Arts Council.
● It creates laws which protect consumers and restrict business organisations from unnecessary exploitation of the consumers.

Central government departments
There are thousands of permanent civil servants in Great Britain and Northern Ireland working in at least 20 different government departments, some of which have some direct or indirect influence or control in the leisure environment, for example:

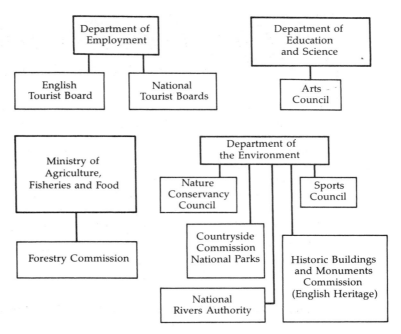

▲ *Figure 5.1   Central government departments and the bodies which work closely with them. All of these affect the leisure environment.*

- **The Department of Education and Science**; under which the Arts Council operates
- **The Department of Employment**; linked to the English Tourist Board and the National Tourist Boards
- **The Ministry of Agriculture, Fisheries and Food**; influences the Forestry Commission
- **The Department of the Environment**; concerns itself with the Nature Conservancy Council, the Countryside Commission (and national parks), National Rivers Authority, British Waterways Board, Historic Buildings and Monuments Commission (English Heritage) and the Sports Council. The Minister of Sport and Recreation is ultimately responsible to the Department of the Environment. (See Figure 5.1.)

Each different government department has diverse responsibilities and is headed by a Minister of State, who is usually responsible to a Secretary of State (who is also a member of the Prime Minister's cabinet) and must account to Parliament for the department's activities. Both the Minister of the department and the Secretary of State are political appointments, i.e. the job holders are appointed by government, and if the government changes its policies, or another political party is elected and a new government is formed, then a new person is elected to the post.

This can have far reaching effects on the leisure and tourism industry, which depends upon the government's political priorities. For example, privatisation policies have been a priority of the Conservative government in the 1980s, therefore ministers in control of departments support these policies and public sector leisure amenities have changed to accommodate these influences. A different government may have different priorities and therefore the people they appoint to ministerial jobs will follow their views.

Since there is a need for some continuity in the administration of these departments many of the personnel working there are permanent job holders, such as the Permanent Secretary, the Deputy Secretary, etc. They do not have to change jobs when the government changes and are said to be 'apolitical' which means that they are supposed to be above (or untouched) by politics, i.e. politically neutral.

Chris Middleton visits a privatised public golf course

The smiling face of privatisation is to be found at Richmond-on-Thames, where three years after taking over two public courses from the Department of the Environment, Golf Course Management Ltd are now recording profits that are well above par.

The courses still remain open to the public; you can still just turn up and play a round of golf, as was intended when the courses opened in 1923 'for the use of the artisan class'. What has changed, however, is that the place is being run by people whose livelihoods depend very directly on the success or otherwise of the courses.

Accordingly, half a million pounds has been spent on improving the quality not only of the greens, but also of the clubhouse, the pro shop – and staff. Nor has this meant widespread sacking of the 'old guard': GCM retained all the existing employees when it took the place over.

'Before, all they had to look forward to was a wage packet that was the same week in, week out, with their union getting them an 8 per cent increase once a year,' says Gilbert Lloyd, the golf-playing half of the two-man GCM partnership. 'Now though, we give them the three P's: a private health scheme, a private pension and, primarily, a good wage packet.'

Promotions manager Paul Moran agrees, pointing to perks like the free weekend in Jersey for the GCM member of staff voted Employee of the Year. 'There's no doubt we have got the incentive to make this place a success,' he says – not least because his father Mike is the other half of the GCM top two.

But whatever the varying motivations for the Richmond staff, there seems little doubt that they have turned a somewhat moribund concern into a thriving enterprise. 'Let's face it,' says Gilbert Lloyd, 'there is always a great demand for public golf courses, so one can always get away with just providing the basics; what we've done, though, is to turn that around and provide the best'.

The result is that the pro shop has expanded seven or eightfold, the staff has grown from 12 to 22, and an astonishing 140 000 rounds of golf per year are played on the two courses.

Not that this is achieved by accident. The GCM policy has been not merely to pack the punters in at random, but to engineer a scientific system whereby the courses are played on not just at peak times but also throughout the 'down' periods, too. Achieving this has involved such diverse activities as persuading Central London hall porters not to send out foreign tourists at peak times, and holding mass pow-wows with various golfing societies in an attempt to lure them to off-peak hours with promises of extra services and convenience.

'Good management, in other words,' says Paul Moran; and the truth of what he says is borne out by the fact that GCM is now being courted by any number of course developers both at home and abroad.

It's a development that is greatly welcomed by Gilbert Lloyd, who admits that he can afford to pay himself a 'generous' salary on the strength of Richmond, but nevertheless holds fast to that most business-like of mottos, which is that 'you don't just stay still – you either get better or worse.'

Article from *Sports and Leisure,*
January/February 1986

ACTIVITY

Read the article above. Check that you know what privatisation means by answering the following questions:

1 Who originally owned the golf course and which sector of the economy did this operate in?

2 Who are the current owners of the golf course and which sector of the economy do they operate in?

3 How has the change of ownership affected the workers in the amenity?

4 Who are the users of the course and what has the change of ownership meant for them?

Nationalised industries (public corporations)

Nationalised industries are enterprises owned and controlled by the state for the benefit of the public. Many nationalised industries have been **privatised**, or 'sold off', to shareholders and now find themselves in the private sector. However, organisations such as the British Broadcasting Corporation (BBC), the Post Office and British Rail continue to be under state control.

The BBC is one of the main promoters of leisure and sporting interests for the population, as it televises and serialises radio and television programmes on different themes, e.g. nature, sports events, cultural and historical events, to appeal to people's interests. Television viewing and listening to radio programmes are passive leisure activities.

British Rail can also be said to support the leisure environment. As a means of communication it enables individuals to travel to various destinations, perhaps as part of a holiday or tourist package. It is also a major landowner in Great Britain and therefore must be concerned with environmental and conservation issues. This in turn affects a whole range of leisure interests such as birdwatching, walking, landscape sketching, architectural appreciation, and so on.

The Post Office tenuously supports the leisure environment by promoting channels of communication between individuals. Although the use of the written word has been superceded by the use of a telephone in many cases, letter writing is still an art. Many friendships and liaisons are continued via the postal system; this is often because there is no adequate alternative form of communication. Stamp collecting itself is a leisure pursuit and in most large Post Offices there is a philately counter for the sale of collectable stamps.

Regional authorities

Regional authorities are government bodies which have been divided, for ease of administration, into areas or regions, for example, regional water authorities, such as Trent Water Authority. Before privatisation the regional water authorities were active in the public sector in promoting leisure pursuits on their inland waterways. Since privatisation they have formed separate companies, operating in the private sector, and each company has different policies for leisure activities and amenities.

Quangos

Some organisations (in particular the Sports and Arts Councils and the Countryside Commission) which are linked to the government departments are known as quangos or Quasi-Autonomous Non-Governmental Organisations. Quangos were created to separate politics from their other roles. For example, the Sports Council was formed to ensure minimum political interference in sporting activities. In practice there are varying degrees of government influence and interference in the running of these organisations.

The four government departments which have the most influence on sports and leisure are:

1 Department of Education and Science
2 Department of Employment
3 Ministry of Agriculture, Fisheries and Food
4 Department of the Environment.

It is acknowledged that, due to the interventions of these departments, leisure policies are fragmented. It is argued that there should be a Minister of Leisure (instead of the Minister of Sport and Recreation) with full responsibility for various aspects of the industry and therefore able to formulate a comprehensive framework for the development of the leisure environment. Others believe that this view would serve to create more interference in the leisure market.

Focus on the Arts Council

The Arts Council of Great Britain was formed in 1964 to continue work begun by the Council for the Encouragement of Music and the Arts with government support.

In 1967 a revised Royal Charter was granted which stated that the Arts Council should have the following objects:

1 to develop and improve the knowledge, understanding and practice of the arts;
2 to increase the accessibility of the arts to the public throughout Great Britain
3 to advise and co-operate with departments of government local authorities and other bodies.

The Arts Council is a publicly accountable body and therefore it has to publish details of its finances. To this end an annual report and accounts are published in order that both Parliament and the general public have an overview of the year's work.

The Arts Council has generally provided revenue or financial support to other organisations on an annual basis. Since 1979 however the Arts Council has suffered severe cuts in its grant provided by Central Government via the Department of Education and Science. This meant that in 1981 the Arts Council substantially reduced its funding to 40 of its client organisations, such as the Regional Arts Associations. Changes in central government policies therefore influence organisations like the Arts Council.

In the 1970s there were changes within the organisation in ideas of what 'art' should be. One of the main problem areas was whether the traditional high arts (e.g. opera, ballet, theatre) should be given greater promotion, or alternatively 'community art' (such as local festivals, carnivals, video, community photography, street murals and drama) should be given greater financial support. Eventually this dilemma was resolved and more publicity has meant that the public have benefited from a greater awareness of the arts.

ACTIVITY

Find out from your local library about your Regional Arts Association:

- Where it is based
- What kind of 'art' it promotes in your area
- Who the decision makers are in your Regional Arts Association.

Focus on the Sports Council

The Sports Council was established in 1972 by Royal Charter and is financed largely through grant aid from the Department of the Environment. It has overall responsibility for sports in England, and has the following aims:

- To promote general understanding of the social importance of sport and recreation.
- To increase the provision of new sports facilities and stimulate existing use.
- To encourage wider participation in sport and physical recreation as a means of enjoying leisure. For example, in recent years the following national campaigns promoted by the Sports Council have targeted specific groups under the banner of 'Sport for All', e.g. Sport for Disabled, 50+ All to Play For, Ever Thought of Sport? (13–24-year-olds), What's Your Sport? (women).
- To raise standards of performance. The Council administers national residential sports centres, with the aim of meeting top level requirements for select sports: Crystal Palace, Lilleshall, Bisham Abbey, Plas y Brenin, Holme Pierrepont.

It also organises residential courses for a variety of sports during the holiday period. These are open to the general public and cater for a variety of levels. In summary, therefore, it promotes excellence and participation in sports.

NB There are separate Sports Councils for Scotland and Wales, with their own logos and different aims.

Structure of the Sports Council in England

The headquarters in London is divided into various units including: Information, Sports Development, Research, Facilities, Technical, Public Affairs, and it produces a bi-monthly magazine. In addition, there are nine regional offices which are responsible for implementing Sports Council policies in the region they serve and for providing a technical and advisory service to local authorities and voluntary organisations. For example, in recent years the Sports Council has been active in promoting the building of **standardised sports centres** (see Chapter 14), and grants have been made available to local authorities wishing to take advantage of the scheme.

Focus on the Central Council for Physical Recreation (CCPR)

This organisation can claim to be 'the voice of sport and recreation'. It represents independent governing bodies of sport, including 87 000 local sports clubs. There is no recognised sport or physical recreation that does not come under the umbrella of the CCPR.

Although this body is not directly linked to a central government department and is an **independent voluntary body**, it receives some funding from the Sports Council. In 1972 the CCPR handed to the government millions of pounds of assets in the form of the six National

Sports Centres, personnel, equipment and cash. In return a legal undertaking was signed with the Sports Council which enables the CCPR to operate and implement new objectives.

Objectives of the CCPR

- To act as a forum where all national governing and representative bodies of sport and recreation may be represented
- To formulate and promote measures to improve and develop sport and physical recreation
- To support work of specialist sports bodies and bring them together with other interested organisations
- To act as a consultative body to the Sports Council and other bodies.

New objectives include the promotion of the interests of its members and analysing current issues such as competitive sport in schools, developing women's sport, financing sport, and promoting the image of British Sport.

The CCPR liaises with the government and local authorities in order to advance sport and recreation in the community. It also acts as an information service on sport and assists in sponsorship schemes between sporting bodies and commercial sponsors.

Organisation of the CCPR

In order to achieve its objectives, the CCPR is organised into six divisions:

1 Games and sports
2 Outdoor pursuits division
3 Major spectator sports division
4 Movement and dance division
5 Water recreation division
6 Interested organisations.

How can CCPR help other organisations?

Member organisations have access to advice on the following:

- Press service
- Sponsorship
- Liaison with government and other local authorities
- Legal advice
- Assistance with fund raising.

CCPR awards

The **Community Sports Leader Award** was created in order to acknowledge the commitment of volunteers to the organisation of sport and recreation in the community. It is designed for people over the age of 16 who wish to acquire confidence and ability in organising groups in games and physical recreation. There are seven units to be covered, including fitness, minor and major games, organising competitions and tournaments, group organisation and first aid. In addition, a period of voluntary work in a coaching/assisting capacity must be undertaken.

The **Basic Expedition Leader Training Award** is also designed for adults over the age of 16 who wish to gain experience in leading groups outdoors.

```
┌─/ ACTIVITY /────────────────────────────────────────────┐
│                                                          │
│  1 Write to one of the following organisations for information:│
│     a) British Tourist Authority                         │
│     b) English Tourist Board                             │
│     c) Countryside Commission                           │
│     d) English Heritage                                 │
│     e) Forestry Commission                             │
│     f) Nature Conservancy Council                      │
│     g) National Rivers Authority.                       │
│                                                          │
│  2 Prepare a short presentation about the organisation, which should include:│
│     ● Background information                            │
│     ● Objectives                                        │
│     ● Role                                              │
│     ● Services.                                         │
│                                                          │
└──────────────────────────────────────────────────────────┘
```

Laws governing the leisure industry

Many laws in England and Wales are formed by statute or Act of Parliament legislation. In this way central government (through Parliament) is responsible for affecting aspects of the leisure industry.

Other government organisations often have special powers delegated to them by central government so that they can form their own laws. For instance, local authorities have special by-laws, e.g. to control the use of their land for caravan sites and other amenities. Nationalised industries also have the power of delegated legislation; for instance, British Rail has certain by-laws which affect the public's use of railway embankments and land it owns.

Licensing laws

Any leisure facility which is used for social and entertainment events needs some form of licence, granted by the police, the courts or the local authority. The types of licences that have to be applied for and granted before trading can take place include the following:

● Entertainment licences
● Theatre licences
● Cinema licences
● Gaming licences
● Copyright licences
● Liquor licences
● Late Night Refreshment House licences, and so on.

Any change the government makes in the licensing laws will have a direct effect on businesses. For instance, the Sunday Trading laws, and the change in the licensing law to allow public houses to extend their hours of business for the sale of alchoic drink, have major repercussions for owners of the businesses: staff are needed to cover the longer hours; increased overheads (such as heating and lighting) result and there is increased competition with similar businesses which may open longer hours. This has to be set against the potential income that may be generated as a direct result of the longer opening hours. The change in the law also has a major effect on the workers in that industry, who may have to endure longer working hours. The customers, on the other hand, may well be the beneficiaries of increased leisure opportunities during the daytime.

Health and safety legislation

There are many different laws which fall under this category, e.g. the Factories Act 1961, Fire Precautions Act 1971, and the Offices Shops and Railways Premises Act 1963. The most recent is the Health and Safety at Work Act 1974. These laws have a direct effect on all business organisations operating in the UK. Any organisation in the leisure or sporting environment must consider the implications for customers, clients, workers, suppliers and owners. The laws give specific details on what kind of safety equipment a business organisation must provide, and what facilities it must offer its employees and customers or clients.

/ACTIVITY/

1 How does the Health and Safety Act 1974 affect you? Find out the details of this Act and note the important features.

2 Why do you think the government believed it was necessary to introduce legislation of this sort?

Consumer law

There are many different laws which fall under this heading, e.g. the Sale of Goods Act, the Consumer Credit Act, and Unfair Trading legislation. The Consumer Protection Act 1987 sought to rationalise these various Acts. The principle aim in consumer law is to protect the customer from unscrupulous retailers and allow for 'reasonable' trade to take place. Any retailer of sports equipment or provider of leisure services must check how consumer law affects them and have up-to-date knowledge of the law.

Employment law

Each employer must be aware of the legislation affecting employment and, in particular, that relating to recruitment, selection and training, contracts of employment, termination (including redundancy), maternity rights, equal pay, and sex and race discrimination.

Public Liability Act

Any premises which the public have access to must be insured for liability that may arise, due to accident or similar occurrence. For example, a sports centre must be insured for public liability insurance up to a minimum sum insured of £250 000. This is necessary in case of an incident, e.g. if a client should slip on a wet floor and suffer injury, the organisation could be sued in court and, if found negligent, would have to pay compensation to the client. In order to ensure that the organisation has funds to cover this eventuality the law states that it must have insurance cover.

Other legislation

There are many Acts of Parliament that refer to specific leisure activities, for example, the 1981 Wildlife and Countryside Act created sites of particular scientific interest (SSIs) and gave some species of animals, birds and plants legal protection.

1 Choose a leisure activity that interests you, from the index in Appendix 1, page 164.

Consult books, newspapers, periodicals, and if possible expert opinion, and find out which particular laws (Acts of Parliament or delegated legislation) affect your chosen activity.

2 Through your research find out the main points of these laws and how they affect your enjoyment of the activity.

Compulsory competitive tendering

In 1987 the government proposed, in a parliamentary bill, that certain services which were traditionally provided by local authorities, e.g. refuse collection, street cleaning, the cleaning of buildings, catering, ground maintenance and vehicle maintenance, should be open to competition. The management of local authority sports and leisure facilities were also to be the subject of **compulsory competitive tendering**. This means that business organisations, or a group of individuals, 'bid' against each other (or compete) to obtain a contract – in this context, a contract to manage a leisure facility. This includes facilities such as sports and leisure centres, swimming pools, golf courses, bowling greens, putting greens, tennis courts, athletics tracks, pitches for team and other games, cycle tracks, water sports facilities, artificial ski slopes, skating rinks, indoor bowling arenas and beaches. The main exclusions would be sports facilities that form part of an educational establishment and are provided mainly for the use of students or pupils.

The idea behind compulsory tendering is that greater competition enables local councils and authorities to achieve better value for money and benefits the communities. However, one point of disagreement is whether the privatised centres would have complete power over the pricing policy for all user groups (this would include traditionally subsidised users such as the unemployed, the elderly and students), or whether the local authorities would retain control over all policy matters. Current employees of the local authorities, known as 'Direct Labour Organisations', may also compete for contracts. If their bids are more competitive than commercial organisations', they may be awarded a contract, usually for a period of five years. Otherwise, Direct Labour Employees may be redeployed by the local authority to any area where there is a labour gap. For example, a recreation assistant could conceivably be redeployed to the Parks and Gardens section.

By 1992 all public sector leisure and sports centres will be subject to compulsory competitive tendering. Each local authority draws up a 'contract' between themselves and the tendering organisation. The onus is therefore on the drafter of the contract (that is the local authority) to make it as watertight as possible in order to protect the consumers of these services. There are far-reaching effects on local councils and authorities, including the standard of leisure provision in different areas, local competition and the charges the consumer must pay for various facilities.

Central government and tax

The state must raise revenue (or money), in order to provide any facility or service for the population. Therefore it has to plan its **fiscal policy** in order to calculate its revenue and balance its expenditure. Fiscal means 'public revenue' and there are many different ways a government can raise revenue or tax from the population. This can affect the leisure industry in one of two main ways:

1 Business organisations may have to pay taxes on their profits direct to central government (direct taxes)
2 Business organisations are delegated to collect certain taxes on behalf of the state and then pay these direct to central government (indirect taxes).

Direct taxes

Direct taxes are those which are collected by the Inland Revenue and are usually levied on income or capital, for example, personal income tax, or corporation tax (levied on profits of companies), petroleum taxes on North Sea oil and gas fields, capital gains tax (on the increased value of an item between the time of its acquisition and subsequent sale), capital transfer tax (a gift tax) and stamp duties (by which certain kinds of legal documents have to be stamped).

Indirect taxes

Indirect taxes are usually collected by the Customs and Excise Department. They are called 'indirect' because the person or organisation actually making the tax payment to the authorities passes the burden of the tax onto another. Such is the case with excise duties on tobacco, alcohol, petrol and diesel and betting. Value Added Tax (VAT) and motor vehicle excise duty are also examples of indirect taxes.

The government also raises revenue from the trading activities of the nationalised industries (public corporations). All this revenue is allocated to central government departments in order to supply certain services like education, nature conservancy, national parks, and amenities such as historic buildings and monuments. Grants and subsidies allocated to the quangos and other leisure bodies are raised in this way.

Central government must allocate finance to local authorities in order that they, too, can provide services. This is known as the Central Government Grant and is discussed in detail in Chapter 6.

/ACTIVITY/

1 How do the independent voluntary bodies interact with the quangos?

2 Give three ways that statutes or Acts of Parliament
   a) restrict
   b) assist
   the leisure and sports centres.

3 a) Explain the difference between direct and indirect tax.
   b) How does taxation affect the leisure industry?
   c) Give examples of various taxes you have paid while pursuing your leisure interests.

Table 5.1

Main landholders in Britain

Central government	Acres
Ministry of Defence	700 000
Ministry of Agriculture, Fisheries and Foods	35 000
Ministry of Transport	150 000
Scottish Office	445 000
Forestry Commission	3 000 000
Nature Conservancy Council	327 000
Other	74 000
Local authorities	
Smallholdings	426 000
Other	476 000
Crown Estate	404 000

Nationalised industries

British Coal	260 000
British Rail	225 000

Other industries

Water supply	293 000

Church of England	172 000

Financial institutes	600 000

Colleges

Oxford and Cambridge	199 000
Other	80 000

Commonland (between 1 100 000 and 1 500 000 – approximation given)   1 300 000

Conservation bodies

National Trust	550 000
National Trust (Scotland)	82 000
Royal Society for the Protection of Birds	180 000
Other	740 000

Private individuals

In **England and Wales** about 200 families own at least 5000 acres each

Duke of Northumberland	91 000
Lord Leverhume	90 000
Earl Lonsdale	69 000
Duke of Devonshire	62 000
Duke of Beaufort	52 000

In **Scotland** 100 families own a quarter of Scotland, nearly 5 million acres

Duke of Buccleugh	277 000
Wills and Estates held in Trust	263 000
Lord Seafield	185 000
Countess of Sutherland	158 000
Duke of Atholl	130 000

ACTIVITY

Refer to the information in Table 5.1 and work through the following tasks:

1 a) Total the amount of land held by central government and add this to the total of land held by nationalised industries.
   b) Total the amount of land held by the conservation bodies.
   c) Total the amount of land held by private individuals and families in England, Wales and Scotland.
   d) Convert these totals to percentages for comparison purposes.

2 How do these percentages compare and what does this indicate about land ownership by central government?

3 How much of this land do you think is used for leisure and recreational purposes by the various organisations?

4 Use these figures as a basis for group discussion.

Remember that these are only the **main** landholders in Britain and that the total amount of land in acres in Britain is approximately 55 000 000 acres. Miscellaneous organisations, small landholders and individuals make up the difference in totals.

Summary

▶ Central government has an important effect on the leisure environment in the UK.
▶ There are four main government departments which influence specific aspects of the leisure and sports industry; they are the Department of Education and Science, the Department of Employment, the Ministry of Agriculture, and the Department of the Environment.
▶ Quangos (Quasi-Autonomous Non-Governmental Organisations) have been created to specialise without direct government influence, e.g. the Sports Council.
▶ Legislation plays a large part in regulating the leisure industry.
▶ Privatisation and compulsory competitive tendering have encouraged the leisure industry to respond to change.

Assignment 3

THE PRIVATISATION DEBATE

Privatisation was one of the most important issues of the 1980s. The whole structure of the public sector has been altered by either the 'selling off' of organisations to shareholders (for example, British Telecom, British Gas and the Water Authorities), or by making these organisations more efficient by the process of compulsory competitive tendering (CCT). Hospitals, public health departments and local amenities are all affected by CCT which means that they must ensure certain parts of their operations (e.g. the catering and domestic cleaning services in hospitals, and the refuse collection of the public health department) are offered for 'tender' by private business organisations. Essentially the business organisation that succeeds in getting the tender should be the one which is most efficient in terms of cost and productivity.

Since the issues are topical there are many sources of information available, such as newspaper articles, TV programmes and documentaries, educational videos, magazine articles, advertising features, company reports and statements, share prices on the stock exchange and so on.

1 Assess the implications of privatisation and compulsory competitive tendering on the following:

a) The government
b) Members of the public
c) The workers in the organisations affected by privatisation or CCT.

The assessment can take place by researching the suggested resources and preparing a set of notes including your views on the subject. For clarity, include the advantages and disadvantages for each group.

2 Using your notes, arrange a debate with members of your group which can be videoed. Organise group members into two opposing sides; those who agree with the privatisation issue and those who have clear arguments against.

If necessary focus the debate on just one issue – for example, what are the benefits and disadvantages of privatising the management of public sports and leisure facilities.

Make sure that each member of the two sides actually puts his or her argument across and there is a chairperson to restrict and stimulate discussion of the points raised.

6 The role of local government in leisure

Aims

▶ To explain the structure of local administration
▶ To describe the different leisure provision of district and county councils
▶ To explain the concept of multiple use facilities
▶ To explain the concept of joint development of local amenities
▶ To illustrate how local authorities raise their funds in order to provide services
▶ To describe in brief the relationship between local authorities and other organisations

Local government administration

If you live in a village or a large town or city in the UK, you may wonder how the local leisure amenities, such as the council-owned parks and gardens, are run. Government decisions concerning these amenities are made at a local level by a body of locally elected people, with the assistance of paid full-time local government officers (the equivalent of civil servants who run the central government bodies).

There are three levels to local administration:

- County councils
- District councils
- Parish councils.

We will look at the most local of these areas of administration first.

Parish councils

A 'parish' or 'community' is an area of rural England and Wales respectively, usually centred around a village or several villages. Originally it was centred around the parish church; the countryside was divided up into parishes so that different areas could administer the Poor Law. Nowadays the parishes are not required to look after their poor residents, but there is plenty of administration at local level to attend to. For instance, most parishes own tracts of land, such as commons or land that is otherwise put to recreational purposes like the local park. The local Parish Councillors meet regularly and attend to ordinary matters relating to the land, e.g. cutting the grass, taking care of the trees and deciding what fees are payable by the local cricket team for use of the green. Parish Councillors may also have to make far-reaching decisions, such as whether to sell land owned by the parish, or they may be consulted regarding certain types of planning permission in the area, e.g. for a new leisure centre or public amenity. Disputes over the routes of local footpaths and bridleways, for example, may involve Parish Councillors, who may work with other local government bodies such as the county councils.

Most parishes employ a Parish Clerk for part-time duties. The Parish Clerk answers the day-to-day correspondence, fixes parish meeting dates, writes up the minutes of meetings and refers matters to the elected parish councillors. Parish councillors work on a voluntary basis, while the Clerk may be paid a salary for his or her work.

Find out more about parish councils and how they administer local recreational amenities.

If you live in a rural area find out:

1 The names of the local Parish Clerk and Parish Councillors. What are their views on the parish-owned recreational facilities available to young people in your area?

2 When do elections to your Parish Council take place? How long is a term of office for a Parish Councillor?

3 What amenities do your Parish Councillors administer? Are there any plans to change these in the future, and if so, how?

4 Compare your answers with other members of the group. How different are the parishes?

If you do not live in a parish or community choose a rural area in your county and conduct some library research on this area, to find out the information required by the above questions.

District councils

A district is an area which exists within a county boundary. It is larger than a parish and may involve many villages, towns, or urban areas. A district council can be a town council, or a city council, or a borough council. All district councils have elected councillors who work with salaried local government officers.

▲ *The Municipal Offices, Cheltenham. The district council provides certain amenities in a locality*

In many regions the political bias of the district council can be different to that of the county council, although of course this may change at local election time. For example, Norwich City Council has had a predominantly Labour-dominated council since the Second World War, in contrast with the Norfolk County Council which has a predominantly Conservative Council.

Obviously the local politics of the region affects the way the council allocates its funds and expenditure, especially to the leisure amenities available. A Labour council may allocate more funding to local amenities and public facilities to enhance the social life of an area for everyone. A Conservative council may provide only basic local authority services so that residents do not have to pay huge charges to the local authority. In these areas there are often more privately owned or joint venture leisure amenities. What services should be provided in the area and how the necessary revenue is raised is decided by local councillors.

County councils

▶
The Shire Hall, Gloucester.
The county council or local
authority has a direct effect on
leisure provision in an area

Counties are the administrative areas within England and Wales, which were created and redefined by the 1972 Local Government Act, updated in 1976.

The following is a summary of the Acts:

- There are 47 counties in England and Wales (39 in England and 8 in Wales).
- Within these counties there are 333 district councils or boroughs (of which 37 are in Wales).
- There are 6 metropolitan borough councils with 36 metropolitan district councils within them.

Local government elections

Elections for County Councillors are different from general elections for Members of Parliament. In central government the Prime Minister decides when the general election will be within a five year period. In local government, elections follow a regular sequence so the Councillors have a fixed term of office. The only exceptions will be if there is a boundary change, or a by-election. A by-election is a mini local election at parish, district or county level, due to a vacancy on the council because of resignation, death or disqualification of a Councillor.

1 Cornwall	55 Antrim
2 Devon	56 Strathclyde
3 Dorset	57 Lothian
4 Hampshire	58 Central
5 West Sussex	59 Fife
6 East Sussex	60 Tayside
7 Kent	61 Grampian
8 Surrey	62 Highland
9 Berkshire	63 Western Isles
10 Wiltshire	
11 Somerset	
12 Avon	
13 Gloucestershire	
14 Oxfordshire	
15 Buckinghamshire	
16 Greater London	
17 Hertfordshire	
18 Essex	
19 Suffolk	
20 Norfolk	
21 Cambridgeshire	
22 Bedfordshire	
23 Leicestershire	
24 Warwick	
25 Hereford and Worcester	
26 Gwent	
27 Mid Glamorgan	
28 West Glamorgan	
29 Dyfed	
30 Powys	
31 Shropshire	
32 West Midlands	
33 Northamptonshire	
34 Lincolnshire	
35 Nottinghamshire	
36 Derbyshire	
37 Staffordshire	
38 Cheshire	
39 Clywd	
40 Gwynedd	
41 Merseyside	
42 Greater Manchester	
43 South Yorkshire	
44 Humberside	
45 North Yorkshire	
46 West Yorkshire	
47 Lancashire	
48 Cumbria	
49 Cleveland	
50 Durham	
51 Tyne and Wear	
52 Northumberland	
53 Borders	
54 Dumfries and Galloway	

▲ *Figure 6.1   Local authority boundaries: Great Britain and Northern Ireland*

District versus county: provision of amenities

The distinction between the services provided by the district council and by the county council is sometimes not entirely clear cut. The main distinction is that the county council deals with broad issues, e.g. education, social services, planning and development, environmental health, highways and transportation and public protection. The district council, on the other hand, deals with more 'local' issues such as refuse collection, improvement grants, rent rebates and allowances, housing, public health, etc.

Some areas of local authority leisure provision, such as museums and art galleries, can be provided by either the district or the county council – there are no hard and fast rules.

Example Upshire is a large rural county. Within the county boundary there is the City of Norcombe, which is the administrative centre. There are three other major towns within the county and at least 20 small market towns. There are a total of seven district councils within the county area, one of which is Norcombe City Council.

Upshire County Council is responsible for the following leisure provision:

- The upkeep and staffing of the city and county libraries
- The upkeep and staffing of four museums within the city boundary and six others within the county
- Giving grants to various sports organisations within the area.

Norcombe City Council administers the following leisure amenities:

- Parks and open spaces within the city boundary
- Allotments
- Two civic halls
- The Tourist Information Centre
- Indoor and other activities including the city swimming pool.

It also gives cultural grants (e.g. to the local art gallery).

As you can see from this example, if you wanted to find out more about local authority leisure amenities in the area you would have to check carefully the responsibilities of the district and the county council. Just because an amenity is in a certain area it does not mean that the local district council is responsible for it.

/**ACTIVITY**/

Find out about your county council and district council leisure provision:

1 If possible visit the offices of both the county council and the local district council. How does their provision of services compare? Draw up a table illustrating what each provides. Are there any areas which overlap?

2 Find out when the local elections for both County Councillors and District Councillors are. Who are your local Councillors? How and when would you consult them?

Amenities for leisure and recreation

Local authorities have a legal 'duty' to provide educational and recreational opportunities for schools, colleges and libraries. In practice they usually take this obligation further and use their discretionary powers to provide facilities on a much wider basis. Different local authorities have differing priorities, and so the facilities offered for leisure and recreation in different local authority areas vary greatly.

Within the Recreation and Amenities Department of a Town Council the following activities may be undertaken:

- Entertainments
- Tourism
- Parks, playing fields and sports grounds
- Cultural activities
- Libraries
- Museums
- Art galleries
- Sports centres
- Swimming pools
- Catering facilities.

The Town Council may provide the buildings, equipment and staff for the amenities, or they may work with the private sector, using 'tendering' to allow private companies to staff or equip the facilities (see page 47).

Multiple use facilities

Since the 1960s central government has urged local authorities to make better and more comprehensive use of facilities (such as sport and educational establishments) in their areas. This is usually done in one of two ways:

Dual use

Both the schools/colleges and the local community share the facilities provided. The pupils and students have sole use during the daytime and term time, and local residents can use the establishments during the evenings and vacations. For example, the adult education evening classes offered to local residents during term time and crêche or play group activities offered during holiday periods.

▶

Shared facilities; a local school is often used by the community for educational courses, social events and sport

Joint use

The school or college and the local community undertake to share and use the facilities during the day and term time, and members of the public can also use the facilities during the vacation times. This promotes a greater use of the facilities, but often the interests of the schools and the members of the public conflict. The Sports Council have taken this idea one stage further and have suggested that if joint use of the amenities is required then there can be either:

a) **integrated facilities:** full integration and use by both students, pupils and members of the public at all times for all the facilities or;

b) **separate facilities:** community facilities are offered to the members of the public, but these are separate to the school or college facilities and amenities. For example, a separate sports and leisure building built on the school site.

⁄ ACTIVITY ⁄

Find out about multiple use in your area.

1 If possible visit two or three of the schools in your area and decide what use they have within the community.

2 Is there a conflict of interests between the local residents and the pupils?

3 Draw up a chart to show the advantages and disadvantages of this joint use from the point of view of the schools' pupils. Next, put yourself in the position of a local resident; how do you think you would feel about this use? What advantages and disadvantages do you think you can suggest about the scheme as a local resident? (Write these down on a seperate chart.)

Joint development or joint provision of local amenities

The concept of joint provision of local amenities was popular in some local authority areas. It meant that both the District Council (or the County Council) worked closely with a private development business organisation to provide certain amenities. For instance, a City Council may want to provide an up-to-date swimming pool in the area, but to do this the Council would have to re-allocate some of its income and give priority to the new swimming pool scheme. However, other priorities, such as provision of new housing or sheltered housing for the elderly, may take precedence.

But wait . . . Thomas Browne Limited, a development firm, want to build a new leisure complex in the area. The plans are submitted, but do not include a swimming pool. With some negotiation there may be scope for the provision of a leisure centre and a swimming pool if the City Council and the developers could work together on the scheme. In this way the Council do not spend a disproportionate amount of money on the swimming pool scheme and can still provide the resources for the new houses and the sheltered housing scheme.

Schemes such as this have enabled areas to have new facilities even when the local Council's resources were limited. However, central government has shown concern over certain joint schemes because negotiations have taken a long time and have re-allocated resources from other priority schemes. In a few cases these schemes have worked against the local residents' interests.

Cost increase puts Parkside project at risk

Despite a Government go-ahead plans to convert Cambridge's Parkside Pool into a tropical-style leisure centre could still be in jeopardy.

And City Council leader, Mark Todd has laid the blame firmly at the door of the Government themselves.

It had taken the Government nine months to decide if the Council plan to allow developers to build an hotel fronting on to Mill Road in return for updating the pool were acceptable, he said.

During that time building costs had been steadily mounting and now the developers were saying the deal would have to be looked at again.

This is not the way for the Government to assist local authorities to provide additional facilities for residents.

'It's a ridiculous way of handling major schemes and it is not the way to encourage either councils to work with the private sector, or for that matter to encourage the private sector to work with councils.

'As I understand it the Government's whole line was that they wanted to encourage more joint development with private enterprise. This is not the way to do it.'

Article from *East Cambridgeshire Town Crier*, 21 January 1989

ACTIVITY

Read the article and answer the following questions.

1 What is the 'Parkside Project'?

2 Who is alleged to have delayed the project and why?

3 What are the consequences of this delay?

4 What are the advantages of ventures of this kind?

How local authorities raise funds

There are three main ways for local authorities to raise funds:

1 The central government grant
2 Municipal trading
3 The community charge and the business rating system.

The central government grant

All local authorities depend on central government to provide grants in order that they may provide facilities and amenities for local residents. During the past few years the amount of income local authorities have received from central government has been reduced drastically – from 60 per cent of their total revenue to 45 per cent in some areas. Therefore the central government grant only goes some way towards funding the provision and upkeep of facilities, and so local authorities must look for additional ways to raise funds.

Municipal trading

There has always been some sort of charge for various local authority-owned amenities. For example, the Council car park charges entrance fees, the local library charges for overdue books, the Council sports centre charges for the use of its equipment.

Recently there has been a greater emphasis on charging entrance and user fees, and each local authority is able to make up some of its revenue by charging consumers for services. Obviously the more the local authority charges, the more it has to compete with private sector organisations offering similar facilities, so it must make sure it provides what the consumer wants – if not it will quickly lose its 'market share'.

Local authority-owned facilities cannot just exist in a vacuum; they need to be aware of their customers and clients. As well as providing a service for the community, they may also make a profit, thus assisting the local authority to balance its budget.

The community charge

Traditionally local rates were imposed on each householder or home occupier in the district and the rates were calculated on the rateable value of each house (or dwelling, such as flat, maisonette, bungalow, etc.) in the area. The Rateable Value (RV) was not the cost of the house or even its selling price, but the value set by the local authority on the amenities its occupiers were said to have at their disposal. For example a large, detached house in its own grounds with central heating, two bathrooms and a conservatory in the south of England might have a RV of £500. A small terraced house in a town with no garden or central heating and only one bathroom may have had an RV of £150.

A local authority may have set a different General Rate charge each year, so in one year if the rate was set at £2 in the £1 Rateable Value this would mean that the person occupying the house with an RV of £500 would have had to pay:

$$£500 \times £2 = £1000 \text{ general rates per year}$$

Assuming the local authority in which the terraced house was built decided on the same General Rate charge (i.e. £2 in the £1 RV), then the occupier of this house would have had to pay:

$$£150 \times £2 = £300 \text{ per year.}$$

The charge was made in half-yearly instalments (in advance) on the 1st October and the 1st April in each year, although most local authorities had various schemes for payment throughout the year.

The introduction of the **community charge** or **poll tax**, which is a charge per head ('poll' meaning 'head'), is easier to understand and varies between local authorities. It is dependent on the amenities available in the area and the central government grant given. Some local authorities have had to impose very high community charges in order to raise enough revenue to provide all the facilities and amenities.

Part of the community charge is a charge for local amenities in your parish. In one area, for example, the community charge is £335.14 per year, and of this amount £16.04 is levied by the parish for certain expenditure.

Read the following article, which clarifies the situation:

How do you feel about
£335.14

Where does your £16.04 Parish Charge go?

The Voice has analysed the precept and expenditure figures presented by the Parish Council on January 8th 1990. This analysis is presented below.

Milton Parish has precepted for £40 000 for the year 1990/91. This figure is divided between approximately 2500 charge payers in the Parish to give a charge of £16.04 per head. This figure is added to the South Cambridgeshire charge to give the final Community Charge which you will be receiving shortly.

The Parish expenditure is expected to be as follows:

Community Centre		£ per Head
Community Centre		
Loan repayment	£18 000	£7.22
1 Support Grant	£8 000	£3.21
Administration		
Clerk's Salary	£2 900	
Stationery	£50	
Photocopying	£350	
Postage/Phone	£130	
Affiliation CALC	£160	
Audit Fee	£200	
	£3 790	£1.52
Village Maintenance		
Grass Cutting	£800	
Cemetery	£820	
2 General Cleaning & repairs	£900	
	£2 520	£1.01
Miscellaneous		
Donations, Xmas Tree etc.	£150	
Bus Passes	£330	
	£480	£0.19
Abnormal Expenditure		
Village Sign	£1 000	
3 Contingency	£5 000	
	£6 000	£2.41
Excess of precept over expenditure	£1 210	£0.49
Total	£40 000	£16.04
Less Adjustment by South Cambs County Council		£2.81
Total Parish contribution to the Community Charge Bill		£13.23

Other Local Parish Charges

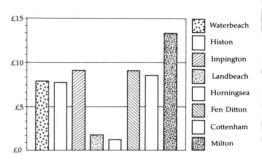

Are You Happy with your Parish Charge?

If you feel that the current expenditure by the Parish Council is excessive or that monies should be distributed to other areas of priority then contact any Councillor.

Areas for consideration

Village Cleaning	**£900**
Support Grant	**£8000**
Photocopying	**£350**
Play School	**£???**
Recreation	**£???**

1 Parish donation to the Community Centre to subsidise the running costs.
2 Includes wages for part time work, collecting rubbish and cleaning bus shelters.
3 To cover potential legal and specialists' fees.

From *Milton Village Voice*, February 1990

The business rating system

Business organisations have also been subject to changes in their rating system and the amount they pay to local authorities for the services they consume. The business rating is now separate from other charges and this also varies from area to area.

Local authorities have therefore been subject to changes in their financial operations. They must ensure that enough revenue is raised from local residents, and by other means, in order to balance their expenditure. They are expected not to overspend their budget.

Local authorities and their relationship with other organisations

There are many ways in which the local authorities can work closely with other organisations in order to finance schemes in their area. Each local authority must carefully prepare its budget, but at the same time still look after the interests of the local residents and compete with the amenities and facilities provided by the private sector.

There are various means by which a council can co-operate and qualify for additional funds. Examples of organisations that provide additional funding are as follows:

The European Community

The European Community via the European Regional Development Fund and the Social Fund provide funds or grants for use in 'deprived areas or regions'. Essentially this is to create jobs in these areas, but a local authority may qualify if it sets up a project to create work and provide further amenities in the area.

Community programmes

A local authority may develop a Community Programme to take this into consideration. There are various projects the Community Programme may be involved in, e.g. in some areas it assists in conservation programmes and urban renovation schemes by creating green areas for wildlife, walkways by canals and rivers and generally tidying derelict areas for everyone's enjoyment.

Central government and enterprise zones

Enterprise zones are areas designated by central government as those areas in which special help is available. This may take the form of grants or subsidies from central government via the local authorities, such as relief from business rates. This in turn attracts new business organisations to an area, and assists them in setting up, e.g. training grants for workers of the organisation which has relocated to the area.

Essentially these schemes are available in certain designated areas which have high unemployment rates. When new businesses are attracted to the area the whole community benefits; potentially there are a greater number of employed people, therefore more wages and salaries are being paid, which in turn can be spent in the local area on goods and services. In this way leisure and tourism are encouraged and areas become more prosperous.

Example

1 Central government gives a grant to a brewery which proposes to invest and start production in an area;
2 The brewery recruits local labour and pays salaries and wages;
3 The salaries and wages become the income of workers who own households in the region;
4 The household income is spent on various goods and services. Some of these goods and services are leisure related, e.g. club membership, sports equipment, entertainment, cinema, theatre;
5 Leisure related business organisations continue to trade and make a profit and use the income from increased sales to hire more staff;
6 With more staff employed there are a greater number of wages and salaries being paid;
7 Wages and salaries are spent on goods and services and so the process continues.

As you can see the government can assist an area by providing funds and this has a 'knock on' effect for the leisure environment.

The Department of the Environment and inner cities development

The Urban Programme is funded by the Department of the Environment and aims to revitalise inner cities. The programme is administered by the Inner Cities Directorate which is part of the Department of the Environment. Local authorities are affected by this scheme because they in turn must assist in its implementation.

Many barren and derelict areas in cities, towns and urban areas have been re-juvenated by the Programme. Overgrown riversides and canal banks have been cleared and walkways created; wasteland lying derelict has been cleared and opened out. Old parks and graveyards have been refurbished and landscaped. The amenities and facilities in the area are therefore improved for public use.

Full of Eastern promise

That's the Romford Ice Rink – council built, privately managed

Andrew Shields explores the partnership

By their very nature local authorities have always been in the people business. Their emphasis though has to be firmly on the people – with 'business' generally meaning how to keep the annual deficit as small as possible.

With private companies, on the other hand, that emphasis is more likely the exact opposite. After all if they don't make a profit they won't last very long.

Into this long standing conflict of attitudes, one of the main reasons for the general wariness by the two sectors of each other, David Price throws a statement which could be of real use in ending the difficulties 'Where there's fun there's money'. It tends to contradict the notion that profit and public provision are incompatible – and maybe points a way forward for a closer relationship.

David Price is managing director of Sports and Leisure Development (S&LD), the people behind the ice rinks at Gillingham and Romford. While the former is owned and operated entirely by the company Romford represents an example of just this kind of new thinking. Havering Borough Council funded the capital costs of the building – about £3.75 million – but handed the management over to S&LD. In return for an agreed rental, the company keeps any profits that the rink makes, up to a certain point at which the Council gets a percentage of further income. What this means, says Price, is that the Council have safeguarded their interests and those of local people and in the end the Borough has a leisure facility for which it only had to meet the capital costs, it runs in effect free of charge for them. It was the success of the South East England rink at Gillingham that attracted Romford to S&LD when they tendered for the scheme. More than 400 000 people skated there in the first year, 1984–1985 and although the emphasis is on getting the public in, the need to cater for serious competition hasn't been overlooked either. The rink employs a group of professional skaters, who are allocated exclusive ice time for teaching. That's a policy which is being repeated at Romford.

Article from *Sport and Leisure* magazine
January/February 1986

ACTIVITY

Read the article 'Full of Eastern promise' and then answer the following questions:

1 Why have most local authorities been good at knowing what the residents of an area want?

2 Are there any traditional differences between private companies and public authorities and their attitudes to leisure amenities? What are they?

3 What possible problems do you think Havering Borough Council envisaged for the Ice Rink Scheme and how did it overcome these?

4 What is the difference between joint provision of amenities and compulsory competitive tendering?

Summary

▶ Local authorities are active in promoting sports, leisure and recreation.
▶ They work closely with other organisations to provide amenities in areas.
▶ These amenities depend on factors such as the parish, district or county political bias, the priority structure that councillors have, and the resources available in the region.

Assignment 4

DRY SKI SLOPE

Westown is a medium sized town with a historical heritage and well-established tourist trade consisting of both domestic and overseas visitors. Recently, two local businessmen have asked for planning permission from the Council to build a £1.2 million dry ski slope and leisure pursuits park on the site of a disused chalk pit in the district known as Springfield.

The plan is to build in two phases, starting with a 230 metre ski slope, the biggest in England, together with an Alpine Ski Lodge, with a club and restaurant. The 20 acre site will have a car park space for 20 cars. Later developments will include a 140 metre long lake for canoeing and sub-aqua, a crèche and nursery, a play area, pets' corner, wildlife nature trail, and toboggan run.

The developers insist that the whole scheme will be kept 'low key' with 60 per cent of the area being devoted to preservation and improvement in the botanical, archaeological, and environmental aspects. Two hundred and fifty thousand pounds have been pledged for these matters. Additionally, the local WildLife Trust and Nature Conservancy Council is going to set up wildlife trails in the parks.

A public meeting has been called to inform all interested parties of the particulars of the scheme, and to give them the opportunity to air their views. Afterwards the 'Hung'* council will vote on whether or not to approve the scheme.

*A 'Hung' council is one where there is no over-riding political majority for any one party.

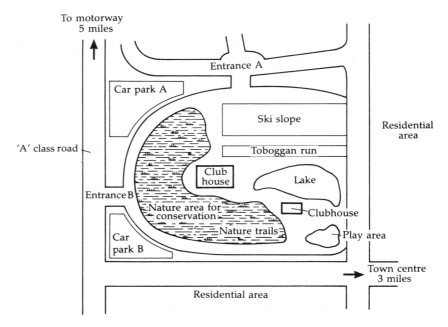

To motorway
5 miles

Entrance A

Car park A

Ski slope

Residential
area

'A' class road

Toboggan run

Club
house

Lake

Entrance B

Nature area for
conservation

Clubhouse

Nature trails

Play area

Car
park B

Town centre
3 miles

Residential area

▲ *Figure 6.2   Plan of Westown dry ski slope complex*

Role play

Allocate the roles to members of your group. Refer to Appendix 2, pages 167–8, for details of your role. Only read the role allocated to you.

- Mayor
- Independent councillors (3)
- Conservative councillors (3)
- Labour councillors (3)
- Local residents
- Lobbyists (environmentalists)
- Journalists
- Local students
- Business developers

/ **ACTIVITY** /

1   Conduct a role play of the public meeting which is chaired by the Mayor. Make sure you put your viewpoint across effectively. Only councillors will be permitted to vote in favour or against the scheme at the conclusion of the meeting. The Mayor will have the casting vote. After the meeting analyse the debate; did the development go ahead? If so, why? If not, why not?

2   Carry out a survey in your area to find out the number of people who have been a) snow skiing and b) dry slope skiing. Is there a connection between participation in the two sports? If there is a dry ski slope near you, find out about the users and their reasons for going there.

3   Imagine that you were one of the journalists present at the local meeting. Draft out the story for the front page, which should include the major issues raised at the meeting, with a summary of the outcome and the implications.

7 / *The private sector and leisure*

Aims

▶ To illustrate the wide range of private sector leisure provision
▶ To illustrate the extent of private sector returns on investment and the profit motive
▶ To show what shareholders expect to gain by investing
▶ To outline the role of shareholders, directors, managers and staff in private sector organisations

Private sector leisure provision

Private sector business organisations add an interesting dimension to leisure provision. They compete with each other to advertise their presence. They are keen to gain customers and clients and use marketing methods to do this. Here are the profiles of six large business organisations that operate in the private sector.

Company profiles

Pontins Limited

Pontins was founded in 1946 by Fred Pontin, who opened his first holiday centre (or 'holiday camp') at Brean Sands near Weston-super-Mare, a popular holiday resort before the Second World War. The idea for this form of holiday caught on and the heyday of the holiday camp was in the 1960s. In 1978 Pontins was sold to Corals and Sir Fred Pontin retired. Corals were taken over by Bass and in 1985 merged the holiday centres with Crest Hotels. In 1987 the holiday centre operation was sold and became Holiday Club Pontin's. This is one of the largest private companies in Britain and has sites throughout the country. It caters for a cross section of users: senior citizens, families, and disabled people. It also targets clubs and societies who use facilities for weekends, conferences and training. Many of the sites are open all year round and they have been upgraded to offer a wide range of popular sport and leisure facilities.

Mecca Leisure Group PLC

Mecca Leisure Group PLC has a broad range of interests including social clubs, night clubs, holidays and catering. There are around 80 social clubs in important towns and cities throughout Britain, which specialise in providing a range of facilities from social drinking to playing bingo. The night clubs are adapted to each region and provide facilities for dancing, eating and drinking. The holidays offered are all UK-based, in holiday villages or hotels. Mecca also offers catering services and has several restaurants in London.

Ladbroke Racing Limited

Ladbroke operates 1700 betting offices in the UK and prides itself in being the largest off-course bookmaker in the world. Its parent company is the Ladbroke Group PLC, which operates Hilton Hotels and Texas Homecare. Ladbroke Racing has over 10 000 employees and is expanding with new betting shops opening throughout Europe. Ladbroke does not confine activities to accepting cash bets on horse racing: it will accept bets on almost anything!

Granada Leisure Limited

Originally known as Granada Theatres, Granada Leisure operated a cinema chain in the 1930s. Today it is part of the Granada Group, with interests in leisure, entertainment, TV rental, music and motorway services. It is a multi-million pound business and operates social clubs, cinemas, bowling centres, night clubs and multi-activity leisure complexes.

Embassy Hotels Limited

In 1961 Ind Coope, Tetley Walker and Ansells became the first national group of brewery companies, known as Allied Breweries until 1981 when they merged with Lyons to become Allied Lyons PLC. Embassy Hotels is part of J. Lyons, the food division of Allied Lyons PLC, one of the largest food and drinks companies in Europe and one of the ten largest companies in the UK. Embassy Hotels runs hotels and leisure centres and aims to attract tourist and business users.

Burger King UK Limited

The Burger King Restaurant chain started in Miami, Florida, USA in 1954. It grew to become The Burger King Corporation and in 1967 became a subsidiary of the Pillsbury Company of Minneapolis. The Burger King Corporation is the second largest fast food hamburger restaurant company in the world, with over 5500 restaurants worldwide and 200 000 company owned and franchised units. Burger King UK Limited is the operating arm of this company in the UK, based mainly in London and the South. The company aims to expand its operations throughout the UK in the future.

These companies have major interests in commercial leisure in the UK and are able to introduce many ideas and trends from abroad. They are commercially successful and earn profits which enable them to influence the demand from the public for leisure services. Many have diversified into different areas of operations; from cinema chains to TV and video rental, brewing to hotel and leisure centres. This spreads the business risk and continues the trend for expansion (known as the market share) of the business.

All the companies have different management styles and operate in different ways; some may have a very aggressive marketing policy, others tend to react more slowly to market forces. However, one aspect of business is vitally important to all: the customer. Without demand from the customer the business would cease trading, so 'customer care' is vital.

Types of business in the leisure industry

The companies illustrated above operate either as **private limited companies** or **public limited companies**. These terms describe their legal status. There are five different legal forms of business operating in the private sector leisure industry. These are:

1 Sole trader
2 Partnership
3 Private limited company
4 Public limited company (PLC)
5 Co-operative.

The main points of each type of business are listed below.

Sole trader

1 The business is owned and controlled by one person. This person takes the risk, provides the capital (perhaps their own savings or a loan), keeps the profits or bears the losses. This is known as unlimited liability.
2 The sole trader is able to employ additional workers if necessary, but is restricted as the business is usually small and cash flow needs careful control.
3 Examples of sole trader enterprises in the leisure environment are self-employed sports trainers, e.g. swimming instructors and football trainers, and retailers of sports and leisure equipment, e.g. shop proprietors and market stallholders.

Partnership

1 A partnership means that the ownership of the business is undertaken by several individuals – by law there must be between 2 and 20 people. Certain professions are excepted from this (e.g. doctors, solicitors and accountants), where a greater number of partners is allowed.

2 Since a partnership involves more than one person, there is usually more capital available, so the business is likely to be larger. The partners can specialise in particular areas if they wish and there is scope for more ideas, and for diversification of the business.

3 Profits have to be shared and so does the decision-making process. The more partners involved in the business the greater the amount of time involved in reaching decisions about the business.

4 All partners of a business are subject to unlimited liability. The exception to this is a 'sleeping partner' who invests in the partnership but has no active role in running the business, and whose liability to debt is limited to the amount of capital they have invested. Each of the partners is bound by the actions of the others, which may cause a problem. For instance one partner might be unreliable and may cause the demise of the business, landing the other partner(s) in debt too.

/ ACTIVITY /

Find an organisation in the area in which you live that is involved in the sports or leisure environment, and that operates as a sole trader (or proprietor) or a partnership. A fitness or beauty centre might be a good example. Arrange an interview with the owner or one of the partners, to ask them a few questions about the business (suggested questions are given below). Compile a report on the business when you have carried out the interview.

Suggested questions
1 The name and address of the business.
2 The name of the owner(s).
3 What the main business activity is – for example, what goods or services they provide.
4 How wide the market is geographically – for example, where clients or customers live.
5 How the products or services are marketed and advertised.
6 If responsibility is delegated to anyone else in the business.
7 If the business employs anyone.
8 What hours of work are completed.
9 If owner(s) can take time off for sickness or holidays, or whether the business has to close down.
10 If there are any plans for expansion.
11 What the advantages of that type of business are, in the owner's opinion.
12 What the disadvantages of their types of business are.

Remember to explain the reason for your interview and to reassure your interviewee that the information will be treated confidentially and is for study purposes only.

Private limited company

1 Any business organisation with the word **limited** in its name implies that investors in the business (or shareholders) are only liable for the company's debts up to the amount of money they have invested. A limited company can be sued in its own name as it has a seperate legal entity, distinct from its owners.

2 In the leisure environment many leisure centres, which have comprehensive facilities and equipment, are private limited companies, formed by a group of acquaintances, friends or

family members. Initial capital is raised through selling 'shares' in the business; further shares can be offered for sale if more capital is required.

3   Because this type of business is a formalised legal arrangement, there are certain laws which apply, such as the Company Acts, and care must be taken in the preparation of accounts and financial dealings. Shares cannot be traded on the Stock Exchange.

Public limited company

Public limited companies can just operate within the UK or as multinationals, operating in several countries. Examples of public limited companies involved in the leisure industry and listed on the Stock Exchange include Grand Metropolitan PLC, Mecca Leisure PLC, Rank Organisation PLC, Trusthouse Forte PLC, Euro Leisure PLC, Granada PLC, Ladbroke PLC, Owners Abroad PLC, Saga PLC, and the Tottenham Football Club PLC. All of these companies are public limited companies and as such must include PLC as part of their name.

1   Because the share prices of these companies are 'quoted' and the shares are sold openly on the Stock Exchange, any member of the public can invest in them.

2   In both public limited companies and private limited companies ownership control is divided between the shareholders who technically own the company (because they have invested the capital) and the controllers who are the board of directors. The directors are voted in by the shareholders, who in turn elect the managers. The directors and managers are trusted by the shareholders to make the best possible decisions for the company.

3   Other investors or companies may wish to make a takeover bid for a public limited company, or aim to merge with it, in which case the board of directors must inform the shareholders, who in turn must vote on the issue.

4   Shareholders can be either ordinary shareholders or preference shareholders. The most commonly quoted prices are for the ordinary shares which allow one vote per share. Ordinary shareholders are entitled to a share of the profits if the company prospers, in the form of dividends. If the company incurs losses, dividends to shareholders are not paid. Being a shareholder is a risky business. Preference shares are not as common as ordinary shares and often carry no voting rights. A preference shareholder gets paid his or her profits (or dividends) at a fixed rate before the ordinary shareholders and so is given 'preference' over other shareholders. In the event of a company incurring losses in any year preference shareholders may be entitled to hold over their claim for dividends until the next more successful year.

Co-operative company

1   This type of company structure is also based on shareholders who own the company. However, the principles involved are more democratic; in a co-operative there is only one vote per shareholder, rather than one vote per share.

2   A co-operative has simple guidelines for its operation. All workers vote in managers and these managers organise the business on behalf of the workers. There should not be a great distinction between a manager or a worker because both can hold shares and both work to the best of their ability to promote the efficiency of the company.

3   Many co-operatives are community orientated. In the leisure environment community organisations such as local art galleries or street theatre/entertainment, may be organised by co-operatives.

Competition in the private sector

Business organisations operating in the private sector have to compete in order to survive. Competition affects all types of business, from the market stall selling antiques and collectors' items to the prestigous golf club in the neighbourhood. In order to compete, businesses must find out who their customers and clients are, i.e. understand *who* is demanding their goods or services. They must also keep up-to-date with who their competitors are and how they market their products and services. Failure to keep up with trends and fashion will have severe repercussions on the business, i.e. losing customers and financial losses.

Investment in the private sector

Investment and ownership of business organisations is more popular than ever before, especially in the booming leisure industry. One of the main reasons for this is because the government has encouraged the setting up of small businesses to alleviate the problems of unemployment in some areas. Investment in company shares has also been encouraged and many people are willing to take the risk, investing funds so that they might be able to reap the rewards of share prices and dividends if the share value increases.

/ACTIVITY/

This activity should be carried out over a period of at least one month. Look at the extract on page 70 from the share index of the newspaper which gives details of the public limited companies in the TV and leisure category. In particular, refer to the column marked 'price'; this is in pence. A (−) or (+) figure means the amount a share has increased or decreased in price over the previous day's trading. The shares referred to are ordinary shares.

1 Choose two of these companies that you have knowledge of, or an interest in. Check their details in the reference section of your library (e.g. shareholders, finance, directors, main operations, subsidiary companies and so on). If possible obtain Company Reports for each of the companies. These are published annually.

2 Check various news items (TV, radio, newspapers) to see if leisure based companies you have chosen have 'made the news' for any reason. See if this has affected the share price and ask yourself why this may be so. Share prices are quoted in the newspapers and on Prestel. Monitor this information over a period of not less than one month and construct a graph of your results.

3 Prepare a report on each of your companies, giving the details that you have researched and the movements of the share prices. Explain the reasons for any fluctuations in share price that have occurred. Give details of shareholders' meetings, company reports on progress, expansion plans, takeovers and mergers. The fluctuations in the ordinary share prices of your chosen companies have a direct relationship with the attractiveness to investors; the higher the share prices the greater the temptation for the owner of the shares to speculate and to sell them and vice versa. The dividends paid on each share (i.e. the entitlement to a share of the company profits) will also affect the share prices.

4 At the end of the time period you will have accumulated information on some leisure based companies operating in the private sector. This can be interpreted with your group and will illustrate how active your chosen public limited companies are in the leisure environment.

1989-90 high	low	stock	price		yld	P/E ratio
		TV & LEISURE				
166	128	Airtours	140−1	xd	6.7	6.72
150	49	Alba	71		8.2	9.57
315	195	Anglia TV	272		4.4	9.74
395	215	Barr WA A	315		7.0	12.69
660	500	Barr WA	660		3.3	26.58
98	13	Bell Group	15		—	—
310	68	Blacks Leis	75e	xd	5.3	9.38
540	225	Boosey & H	450		3.1	17.13
420	317	Brent Walke	375+7		4.3	7.57
283	127	Capital Rad	244−1		2.5	17.18
954	660	Carlton Com	786+17		1.6	14.77
823	578	Central TV	773+8		4.7	11.52
243	123	Chrysalis	146		3.7	—
150	$50\frac{1}{2}$	Cityvision	140+4		0.5	34.70
392	280	Compass	375+1		3.2	15.18
99	66	European Le	90+3		2.0	—
£11$\frac{7}{8}$	740	Euro Disney	£11$\frac{3}{16}$+0$\frac{3}{16}$		—	—
247	149	First Leisu	232		2.1	16.98
74	45	Grampian TV	71		5.8	8.10
396	270	Granada	328		5.0	10.28
142	103	Granada 7hp	120+1		8.3	—
136	84	HTV Gp N/V	132+1		5.1	8.37
88	78	LWT CP	87+1		6.0	—
352	213	Ladbroke	306−6		3.9	15.89
111	19	Leisure Inv	19−1		7.7	17.27
200	147	Mecca	151+0$\frac{1}{2}$		4.0	15.66
102	52	MY Hldgs	56		2.0	—
87	49	Owners Abd	61+1		5.4	7.91
230	72	Pavilion	74−2	xd	8.1	5.74
590	295	Photo-Me	350		1.1	25.14
250	183	Pickwick	249		1.9	24.78
319	135	Quadrant	143		3.6	9.40
690	174	Rly Useful	232+4		9.8	26.85
306	199	Saga	297+1		2.6	33.00
518	368	Scot TV	514+4		5.3	9.00
282	197	Stanley	236	xd	2.7	14.43
98	65	TSW T/V SW	90		6.1	7.26
347	145	TVS Ent	146+1		13.0	3.89
579	360	Thames TV	544+2		3.8	11.81
896	625	THORN EMI	772+8	xd	4.8	12.05
147	95	Tottenham H	116		5.8	20.60
476	348	Tyne Tees	369+1		6.6	6.91
152	90	Ulster TV	145		5.5	8.83
100	66	Video Magic	86−1	xr	—	17.55
129	85	Wembley	102−0$\frac{1}{2}$		2.4	15.62
313	225	William Sin	250ir		2.8	18.10
327	222	Yorks TV	294	xd	5.1	8.94
185	138	Zetters	152	xd	5.5	21.47

▲ *Extract from ordinary share prices in a newspaper: TV and leisure section*

Summary

▶ There are five main legal forms of business which operate in the private sector; they range from self-employed individuals such as sports trainers, to large multinational companies like fast food chains.

▶ The overall image of private sector organisations is lively and adaptable, primarily because they must adapt to new trends and market forces in order to survive.

▶ Customer care is vital in private sector business organisations due to the necessity of competing with other operators for demand for products and services.

- Larger organisations that operate in the private sector have different styles of management which affect their image and how they market their products or services, e.g. aggressive expansion policies owe a great deal to certain management techniques.
- Companies in this sector have shareholders who have a vested interest in the companies' financial operations. They expect dividends and stable or rising values of share prices.
- Without these they may withdraw their funds and the company would have to look elsewhere for capital.

Interview analysis sheet

Complete **one** of these sheets for **each** of the organisations visited.

Section 1

Organisation ....

Address ....

Contact name ....

Position held/title ....

Date of interview ....

Time of interview ....

Section 2

Questions that you propose to ask:

Section 3

Evaluation of the interview:

Duration of the interview .... minutes

Consider the following points: communication, helpfulness and relevance of responses for the purpose of the interview and in response to the questions asked.

▲ *Figure 7.1   Interview analysis sheet for Assignment 5, page 72*

NB If you are unable to arrange an interview with someone from one of your chosen organisations, visit your local library and conduct some desk research. If the private sector organisation is a PLC then details of ownership and finance will have been published. You may be able to obtain a Company Report.

The local authority should have details of the public sector organisation.

Assignment 5

COMPARISON OF BUSINESS ORGANISATIONS IN THE PUBLIC AND PRIVATE SECTORS

Choose two similar types of leisure organisation, one which operates in the public sector and one in the private sector, from the area in which you live. Complete the following tasks:

1 Arrange an interview with a manager or director at each of the two organisations you have chosen.

2 Complete the interview analysis sheets (see page 71 for draft).

3 Produce a report which compares the two organisations and the facilities they offer.

The report should include the following:

a) The aims and objectives and type of ownership of the organisations.
b) Indications of the capital investment, running costs, and profitability of the organisation.
c) Membership and user profiles, numbers of members, conditions or rules of membership, provision for disabled users.
d) The range of services or goods offered by the organisations including social activities and seasonal variations and special events.
e) The location of the premises and layout.
f) Details of how the organisations promote and advertise themselves.
g) Details of the staff employed so that an organisation chart can be drawn up showing the management structure.

8 Voluntary bodies and the leisure industry

Aims

▶ To explain the structure of voluntary bodies
▶ To give examples of the range of voluntary bodies
▶ To explore the sources of funding of voluntary bodies
▶ To show how voluntary organistions 'fit in' to the leisure environment

The structure of voluntary bodies

A voluntary body literally means a group of people who freely consent to join an organisation like a club, society or association. This organisation does not fall neatly into the public or the private sector of the economy because it is neither state-owned or controlled, or purely controlled by an individual or group of people for profit (see Chapters 5, 6 and 7).

Voluntary organisations exist for the benefit of their members and supplement the facilities, services and activities of both the public and the private sector organisations.

The majority of voluntary organisations are formed by people so that they can meet certain needs. For example a group of like-minded people may decide to form a drama group because one does not exist in their area. The local authority may well provide financial assistance indirectly to the drama group by allowing the group to use the Community Centre at a reduced cost.

Voluntary organisations are started up by for specific purposes:

1 They meet a specific need, e.g. a tennis club.

2 They encourage recreation, i.e. relaxation rather than work.

3 They provide opportunities for people to pursue leisure activities; these may be active, passive, sporting or non-sporting activities.

4 They enable thousands of people to give service to others, e.g. The Red Cross and hospital visiting.

5 They have a pioneering role because they set up organisations that would otherwise not exist, e.g. the drama group mentioned above.

6 Their main aim is not commercial activity based on a profit motive, although some of them may use commercial activities (shops, restaurants or mail order catalogues) to generate public interest, e.g. the Royal Society for the Protection of Birds and The National Trust.

There are a wide variety of these voluntary organisations, ranging from small scale local groups with under 20 members (for instance a youth club) to large scale national and international organisations, such as the Youth Hostel Association.

Fund raising

As mentioned above, voluntary organisations are not primarily profit orientated and funds are raised in any of the following ways:

1 Grants from central government and local government.
2 Subscriptions from members.
3 Fund raising events, e.g. barbeques, fêtes, jumble sales.
4 Donations and gifts from people or other organisations, e.g. money or estates left by people in their wills.
5 Fees that are charged for certain services provided, e.g. entrance fees.
6 Sponsorship by certain individuals or organisations, e.g. the Ford Motor Company supporting the National Trust.

Relationship with government bodies

An indirect link between voluntary organisations and central government exists in that funds are awarded to government-linked bodies (such as the Sports Council) in the form of grants, which are then channelled into the voluntary sector organisations. The Arts Council may use some of its annual grant from central government for the purpose of renovating a drama centre.

The following government bodies may award subsidies or grants to voluntary organisations:

- The Sports Council
- Development Corporations
- Community Industries Limited
- European Community
- Department of Education and Science
- Home Office
- Department of Social Security
- English Tourist Board
- Arts Council of Great Britain
- Countryside Commission
- National Council of Voluntary Organisations
- Department of the Environment
- Department of Employment.

From the newspaper cutting you will see that local authorities also award grants and subsidies to voluntary organisations, who spend these funds on their own projects or running expenses.

Voluntary groups get cash lifeline

Voluntary groups in Cambridge have been thrown a £162 673 lifeline by a county council committee.

As part of the county's annual grants bonanza, 33 city organisations have been awarded cash by the Social Services Resources Subcomittee.

Dozens more organisations in the city are also set to benefit.

The largest grant given by the committee was £32 900 to Crossroads, which provides relief workers to allow people looking after long-term sick relatives the chance of taking a holiday.

One of the smaller amounts was £1000 to the Cambridge Society for the Blind.

Altogether nearly £650 000 was approved for groups throughout Cambridgeshire, including Crossroads at Huntingdon (£28 260), the St Ives Day Centre (£9000), and Ely and District Family Support Scheme (£3927).

However, a grant of £15 500 requested by the Centre 33 project for counselling young people is still being considered by officials and will come before councillors in April.

Article from *Cambridge Evening News*
1988

The range of voluntary organisations

Voluntary organisations are extremely varied in the range of activities they cover. As well as the national organisations already mentioned above, there are also many local ones, which fall into these categories:

- **Community action groups**   These exist either to get something done in an area (e.g. to pressure local government into diverting traffic from a town centre) or to provide facilities that would not otherwise exist for some sector of the population, e.g. Gingerbread, an organisation for one-parent families.
- **Youth organisations**   These are formed specifically for 'young people' in order to provide them with certain facilities. There is some discrepancy over what constitutes a young person; some organisations allow teenagers to join (i.e. those aged between 13 and 19 years old), others state a person is still 'young' up to the age of 30! The Young Men's Christian Association (YMCA) provides facilities for lodgings, sport and recreation, the National Association of Youth Clubs provides facilities in a neighbourhood like a meeting room, pool and table tennis tables. The Scouts and the Guides also fall into this category.
- **Disabled groups**   These are for disabled people with physical or mental disabilities of varying degrees of severity, e.g. Disabled Drivers Motoring Clubs.
- **Adventure organisations**   Not for the faint-hearted, these are for outdoor recreation both here and abroad, e.g. The Duke of Edinburgh's Award Scheme, Outward Bound, Operation Raleigh.
- **Sport and physical recreation**   These are designed to promote physical fitness and specific sporting activities, e.g. Keep Fit, The National Skating Association of Great Britain and British Octopush Association.
- **Animal and pet groups**   These have been formed to protect and promote certain types of pet (e.g. The Cats Protection League). Some organisations in this category involve sporting events and animals, for example, the Pony Club.
- **Environmental, conservation and heritage groups**   These organisations are designed to protect the environment, e.g. the National Trust, Friends of the Earth and the Royal Society for the Protection of Birds.

- **Counselling organisations** These assist people with problems and queries on general and specific matters, e.g. the Citizens Advice Bureaux, Alcoholics Anonymous, Marriage Guidance Council, Samaritans, and the Aids Helpline.

All voluntary organisations in the categories mentioned may well be members of the National Council of Voluntary Organisations (NCVO). This organisation protects the interests of voluntary bodies in general and draws its members from voluntary groups concerned with recreation, the environment and social problems. The NCVO publishes material for the benefit of its members which give professional advice and support. The NCVO has obtained charity status itself and thus raises money to continue to help its members.

The internal structure of voluntary organisations

Employees

Most of the national voluntary organisations like the National Trust or The Royal Society for the Protection of Birds employ a vast number of salaried professionals in the head offices, regional offices and branch offices throughout the country. These people may have management or administrative jobs or have technical knowledge, and have been recruited because they have some kind of skill, e.g. an art historian, or a botanist.

Many local voluntary organisations may depend entirely on the voluntary service of people in order to run their day-to-day activities. This involves interested people giving their labour for no monetary gain. An example of this is a driver for the Hospital Car Service (an organisation which ferries patients to and from hospital), who gets paid a petrol allowance but no salary or wage. Many people who undertake these voluntary duties do so because they get a personal feeling of satisfaction from doing them. Others, for instance Scout and Guide leaders, undertake the organising because they personally enjoy the tasks they set themselves.

Honorary members

These are invitations given to certain people esteemed by the voluntary organisation for past services or financial contributions to the organisation. Professor Brown, an eminent historian, may be invited to become an honorary member of a local historical society, giving the organisation credibility and endorsing its activities.

Ordinary members

These are members of the general public who are interested enough to pay a subscription to the voluntary organisation in return for membership. With national societies this involves an annual sum of money and may entitle a member to a members' magazine, a handbook, up-to-date reports and so on. Often membership can be taken out for life, or for the family, at certain reduced rates of payment. If a Deed of Covenant is signed by a member this entitles the voluntary organisation to claim back tax relief from the Inland Revenue on the subscription, which in turn increases the funds of the voluntary organisation.

Patrons

These are people who are invited to become linked with the voluntary organisation, usually because there is some prestige value to their involvement. It is general practice for the patron's name to be printed on membership forms and publicity documents. Patrons may have given a substantial financial donation to the organisation, or may just be interested in the work of a particular organisation (for example Princess Diana and the London Festival of Ballet).

The case study on the National Trust that follows illustrates certain characteristics of national voluntary organisations. These are sources of funding, the importance of marketing and market research and the necessity to recruit new members.

Focus on the National Trust

The National Trust is a large national voluntary organisation, and is a registered charity. By registering with the government as a charity the organisation becomes exempt from paying tax on its earnings and pays only 50 per cent of its general rates bill to the local authority where it is based.

The National Trust exists for the benefit of the public and holds countryside and buildings in England, Wales and Northern Ireland in 'trust' for future generations of people. Although it is independent from the government it works on behalf of the nation with the support and recognition of central government in England, Wales and Northern Ireland. The National Trust in Scotland is a separate organisation and operates independently of the English based organisation illustrated here.

The National Trust derives an income from the following sources (see also Figure 8.1):

1 Property and financial donations from individuals and from business organisations.
2 1.3 million ordinary members who pay subscriptions.
3 Grants from government organisations or statutory bodies.
4 Fees from visitors.
5 Gifts and legacies from individuals.
6 Sponsorship from business organisations.
7 Pledges and Give as You Earn: this is a scheme by which people sign a covenant or form to guarantee that they will allow a certain amount of money to be deducted from their earnings which will be handed over to the charity or voluntary organisation by their employers. Donations or gifts to these charities are deducted from an employee's wage or salary by the employer who hands it over to the charity or charities of the employee's choice. The employee gets tax relief on the amount deducted of up to £120.00 per year.
8 National Trust Enterprises: this is responsible for commercial activities such as gift shops, tea shops, mail order catalogue and various other profit making events. The company does not enjoy exemption from tax unlike most of the National Trust income, although the surplus income from these activities is donated to the Trust by a Deed of Covenant.

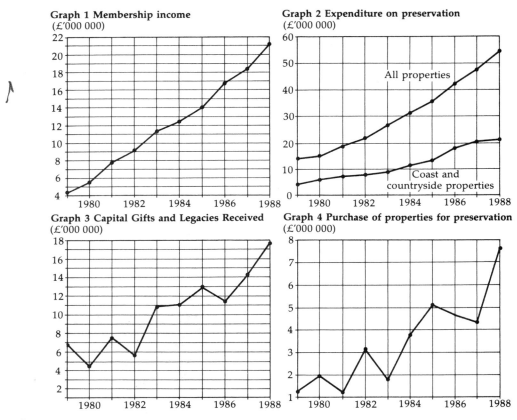

Graph 1 Membership income
(£'000 000)

Graph 2 Expenditure on preservation
(£'000 000)
All properties
Coast and countryside properties

Graph 3 Capital Gifts and Legacies Received
(£'000 000)

Graph 4 Purchase of properties for preservation
(£'000 000)

▲ *Figure 8.1   National Trust income and expenditure*

Historical aspects of the National Trust

The Trust was founded in 1895 by three people who foresaw an increasing threat to the countryside and ancient buildings of England, Wales and Northern Ireland.

Originally the Trust was a public company, but in 1907 the Trust was incorporated by Act of Parliament with a mandate to promote 'the permanent preservation for the benefit of the nation of lands and tenements including buildings of beauty or historic interest'.

The Act's crucial provision granted the Trust its unique power to declare its property **inalienable**, meaning that National Trust property can never be sold or mortgaged.

In 1937 a further Act of Parliament enabled the National Trust to hold country houses and contents as well as land and ancient buildings. This led to the Country House Scheme by which a house, with or without its contents, may be presented to the Trust with a financial endowment to maintain it in perpetuity. In return the donor and their family may go on living in the house subject to public access and measures to maintain the essential character of the property.

The National Trust is highly selective; it aims to preserve houses as homes, not museums, if possible lived in by the families traditionally associated with them. It now owns 190 houses; some are associated with such famous people as Sir Francis Drake (Buckland Abbey, Yelverton, Devon), and Thomas Hardy (Hardy's Cottage, Higher Bockhampton, Dorchester, Dorset).

The National Trust is a registered charity; its property can only be leased with the approval of the Charity Commissioners. The trust continues to use its funds to acquire and preserve beautiful and historic buildings and places. Often the Trust works in conjunction with the local authority in the area in order to carry out its work (e.g. Buckland Abbey and Plymouth City Council).

The Trust as a landowner

1 The National Trust is the country's largest private landowner. It owns 550 000 acres, including gardens, villages, farms, woodland, antiquities (such as a sizeable part of Hadrian's Wall), nature reserves (e.g. Wicken Fen) and coastline.

In 1965 it undertook a special conservation measure to extend protection over the coastline. A survey showed that one third of the 3000 mile coastline was of outstanding natural beauty and worthy of permanent preservation. In May 1965 the Duke of Edinburgh launched Enterprise Neptune, the most ambitious conservation project ever undertaken in Britain.

Objectives of Enterprise Neptune

- To acquire and preserve fine coastline
- To improve the quality of the National Trust's existing coastline by careful management
- To focus public attention on the problem of coastal development
- To raise an initial sum of £2 million

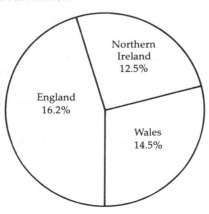

Figure 8.2
The percentage of coastline under
National Trust protection

```
National Trust Administration

            ↕

Head Office (London) executive staff

            ↕

        16 regional offices
               in
    England, Wales and Northern Ireland
    run by Regional Information officers (RIO's)
```

Figure 8.3
National Trust
administration

Policy making by the National Trust

This is carried out by the Trust's Council of 52 members. They are nominated by institutions such as the British Museum, the Rambler's Association and the Royal Horticultural Society. Half the number of members are elected by the Trust members at their Annual General Meeting.

Figure 8.4
National Trust
Council structure

The main committees are shown in Figure 8.4 and have different responsibilities.

All committee members are volunteers and have a variety of business skills and expertise.

The National Trust works closely with other national and local bodies concerned with conservation and planning in order to try to ensure that their work is environmentally sound. The main bodies that it works with are shown in Figure 8.5.

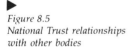

Figure 8.5
National Trust relationships
with other bodies

The National Trust runs volunteer groups, called Acorn Camps, which allow young people to undertake projects in England, Wales and Northern Ireland specifically for conservation of the environment.

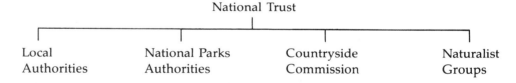

ARE YOU FIT AND DO YOU ENJOY WORKING IN
A FRIENDLY CLOSE-KNIT ATMOSPHERE?

DO YOU FANCY A WEEK IN THE OUTDOORS FOR AROUND £20.00?

THEN SEND FOR THE NATIONAL TRUST ACORN CAMP BROCHURE

THE NATIONAL TRUST VOLUNTEER UNIT
PO BOX 12
WESTBURY
WILTSHIRE
BA13 4NA

Figure 8.6
National Trust advertisement
for Acorn camps

80

▲ *Acorn Camps: volunteers involved in conservation and the environment for the National Trust at Stourhead, Wiltshire*

Case study: Wimpole Hall

The case study that follows is based on one of the National Trust properties: Wimpole Hall in Cambridgeshire. The Hall is an eighteenth century style building and is of interest for its 350 acre landscaped park. The site includes a working farm (Home Farm), a restored Victorian stableblock with heavy horses, parklands (including a folly and a Chinese bridge) and woodland areas.

The Regional Information Officer on the site was interviewed by a student of leisure studies in order to find out if the students could assist the Trust by carrying out any survey work at the site.

The following is a transcript of the interview between the student and the Regional Information Officer (RIO):

Student   How do you go about marketing the estate?

RIO   We advertise widely through the local and regional press including radio, holiday guides, Tourist Board publications and leisure magazines. Actually, we employ an agency for the marketing side.

Student   I see. Judging from the number of attractions here, you seem to be aiming at a family market.

RIO   Oh yes, we have Suffolk Punch Horses and waggon ride trails, a cafe, shop, then there's the farm and the Victorian stable block which is being renovated at present. Out of season we try to attract visitors back with a full programme of events, such as concerts and gourmet evenings.

Student   How much do you know about the visitors to Wimpole Hall?

RIO   Well, we've never really carried out market research, but we would like to know a lot more about our visitors. It would really help our marketing strategy.

Student   In that respect we could probably be of help. What sort of information would you like to know about your visitors?

RIO   Well, where they came from for a start. Also why they come and if they're members of the National Trust. I think we need to know about pricing structure; if they feel it's value for money; would visitors be prepared to pay a moderate access charge?

Student	Er, what does that mean exactly?
RIO	Well for the use of the car park, toilets, shop, etc.
Student	Oh yes, and what about improvements?
RIO	Yes, it's important to find out what they think about that. Also we must know how they heard about us. We'd like to know how effective our advertising is.
Student	And is social stratification important – you know, what their occupation is and how old they are, whether they have children and so on?
RIO	Yes, because it'll help us to target our marketing more accurately.
Student	Well, I think from the information you have given me, we could draft a questionnaire and send it to you for approval. How about that?

ACTIVITY

1 From the dialogue write the minutes of the meeting that took place.

2 Design a questionnaire based on the objectives given by the Regional Information Officer.

3 You are given the following information regarding the staff of Wimpole Hall:

a) **The hall**
Administrator: responsible for all aspects of public access and presentation of the property;
Custodian: responsible for the contents of the house, day-to-day cleaning and maintenance: answers to the Administrator;
Cleaners (4): responsible to Custodian, mornings only and occasional evenings;
Secretary: administration of office, including public bookings, responsible to the Administrator.

b) **The garden**
Gardener-in-charge: responsible to Administrator on all but technical matters;
Assistant gardener: responsible to Gardener-in-charge;

c) **The park**
Estate Warden: responsible to Administrator in all but technical matters, maintenance of woodlands, trees, recreational areas and park walks;
Assistant Estate Warden: responsible to Warden.

d) **The farm**
Land Agent: responsible for all matters pertaining to the farm estate and associated property: farmland, woods, farm cottages, etc.
Farm Manager: responsible to Land Agent for farming matters; close liaison with Administrator over access to farm;
Farm Secretary: farm administration, stock records, ordering;
Tractor driver
Stockman
Small animals stockman
Shepherd } all responsible to Farm Manager.
Horse handler
Stable hands (2)

e) **Visitor services**
Shop manager: responsible to Administrator on day-to-day matters and to Regional Trading Manager for merchandise matters;
Shop Assistants (2): responsible to Shop Manager;
Catering Manager: responsible to Administrator on day-to-day matters;
Cook: responsible to Catering Manager.
Seasonal counter staff (4–6)
Ticket sellers

Car park attendants – casual workers
Farm receptionists (2)
Information assistants (part time)
Ice cream seller – casual work

The information given must be divided up into the following departments:
Estate
Farm
Shop
Catering
Garden.

Draw up an organisation chart of Wimpole Hall. Be prepared to justify the choices that you make as you arrange the chart.

4 Find out who your Regional Information Officer for the National Trust is. Contact him or her with a view to carrying out a visitor survey for a National Trust property in your area. (See Assignment 11, page 143).

5 You are a trainee marketing assistant with the National Trust and you have been asked to talk to students at a local college about the contemporary administrative structure and current activities (such as Enterprise Neptune and Acorn Camps). Plan your talk and make it as interesting as possible, with visual aids.

▲ Wimpole Hall, Cambridgeshire

Case study: West Winton Tennis Club

West Winton Tennis Club

Welcomes new members
for the forthcoming season

All welcome
Beginners to experts

Contact
The Membership Secretary
Tel. 32650
for further details

▲ *Figure 8.7   West Winton Tennis Club advertisement*

The above advertisement was printed in a local newspaper. When you contacted the Membership Secretary to apply to join the club, he just kept on talking! The one-sided telephone conversation went on for ages! You couldn't just put the telephone down, but had to listen to all the facts about the club. The Membership Secretary was obviously concerned about the Club and desperate for members.

The following details are a summary of what you were told:

The annual cost of subscription for senior members is £15; for those under 16 years of age the subscription is £10. There is also a scheme for family membership at a cost of £25 per family.

The club provides two asphalt courts, which are actually owned by the local Parish Council. A wooden shelter is also provided for members waiting to play on the courts. Members of the tennis club could use these courts at any time, but in the event of great demand on any particular day or evening the members are expected to play doubles, rather than singles.

On Monday nights during the summer season, weather permitting, tennis coaching is given to young members at no extra charge. Obviously this restricts the availability of the courts for the senior members. On Thursday evenings during the summer season, weather permitting, coaching is available to senior players at a nominal charge of 50 pence per session.

The total number of paid up individual senior members for the previous year was 107; the junior members total was 55 and family membership subscriptions totalled some 30 families of various sizes.

Although the courts are owned by the Parish Council and the tennis club pays a nominal rent of £30 per annum, the Tennis Club has full responsibility for maintenance and upkeep of the facilities. Last year the club managed to purchase two new nets and had to maintain the shelter which needed repair and weather proofing.

Next year the club hopes to re-asphalt the two courts, at a cost of over £2000, but in order to do this it must increase membership and run some social events to generate an excess of income over expenditure.

The Membership Secretary eventually agrees to send you a form to complete (you feel morally obliged to join now after hearing about the lack of funds!). When you receive the form you see that he has also included the financial details from last year.

```
West Winton Tennis Club
Receipts and Payments Account for the year ended 30.4.88

Balance b/f          £10.00        Rent                    £30.00
Membership                         Nets                  £1000.00
   fees            £2905.00        Repairs                £900.00
                                   New balls               £80.00
                                   League fees             £50.00
                                   Refreshments            £20.00
                                   Donation to
                                      charity             £100.00
                                   Coaching fees          £500.00
                                   Transport
                                      costs               £200.00
                                   Groundsman             £500.00
                                   Insurance              £250.00
                                   Administration
                                      charges             £150.00
Excess of
expenditure
over income       £865.00
                  _____                                _____
                 £3780.00                                £3780.00
```

▲ *Figure 8.8   West Winton Tennis Club Receipts and Payments Account*

Please note that this is a Receipts and Payments Account. The Membership Secretary did not send you either the Income and Expenditure Account or the Balance Sheet for the past year.

/ACTIVITY/

1 **Group work**
   As a member of the Tennis Club you have been voted onto the committee. The following roles are to be assigned to members of your group:
   ● Treasurer
   ● Assistant Treasurer
   ● Chairperson
   ● Secretary
   ● Fixtures Secretary
   ● Coach
   ● Junior Representative
   ● Club Members.
   (Refer to Appendix 2, page 168 for brief descriptions of these roles.)

   At the Club's Annual General Meeting, it is to be decided how to raise the necessary finance for the renovation programme. You need to decide which fund-raising social events appeal to most members and which must be organised. The Club Committee should lead the discussion, but remember that valid ideas come from club members. All suggestions must be minuted by the Secretary and fully discussed at the meeting. The Club Treasurer and Assistant will be expected to refer to the financial costings in the text.

   At the end of the meeting bring the subjects discussed to a vote; once your club has decided its policy for this year move to **Task 2**.

2 Assuming that you have decided on various fund raising events, divide into smaller groups and plan a strategy for one of the events. A written summary of the strategy discussed should be submitted to the Club at a follow-up meeting next week. The details to be agreed upon must include the following:

- the nature of the event
- date
- time
- cost
- venue
- legal requirements (e.g. for licensing and publicity). (Refer to Chapter 5.)

3 Design some form of publicity material for the event your group has chosen. This might take the form of a poster or handbill. The use of colour is important in this activity.

▶
Volunteer working for MENCAP

/ **ACTIVITY** /

Test your knowledge on this chapter.

1 List three sources of finance for voluntary organisations.
2 What are the main aims and objectives of voluntary organisations?
3 Who are voluntary organisations accountable to? (Give two examples.)
4 Why do voluntary organisations hold general meetings?
5 How does central government assist voluntary bodies in the UK?

Summary

▶ Voluntary bodies can be international, national, or local organisations.
▶ Voluntary organisations sometimes have charity status and receive tax relief and reduced local authority rates. They are not expected to make a profit but to balance their accounts.
▶ Some of them are subsidised by central and local government grants, and they are all accountable for their financial dealings – to their members, the Charity Commissioners, the government and so on.
▶ Membership is voluntary and comprises like-minded individuals involved in activities.
▶ Voluntary organisations hold general meetings to advise members of policy decisions and to get ideas for the progression of the organisation. Officers are also elected at Annual General Meetings. Some of these officers have honorary status.

VOLUNTARY BODIES

1 Choose a voluntary organisation and prepare a ten minute presentation for the group outlining the aims, activities, development, membership profile, etc. Produce one A4 sheet handout for each member of the group giving the main details of the organisation you have chosen.
You may use an overhead projector as necessary.

2 Produce a brochure for the organisation with the aim of attracting new members. It should include:
   a) Introduction, purpose and role, development, profile of any important personalities connected with the organisation or endorsing it;
   b) Organisation chart;
   c) Description of activities;
   d) Membership details;
   e) An outline of the ways in which funds are raised and how the organisation publicises itself.

3 a) Conduct a survey of the publicity material of five different local voluntary organisations in your area, e.g. newspapers, posters, leaflets, etc.
   b) Compare the literature in terms of quality and quantity of information, the marketing appeal, illustrations, appropriate use of language and display areas.
   c) Evaluate which organisations appear to be more successful with the publicity they produce.

Who uses leisure facilities?

Aims

▶ To identify ways of categorising user groups
▶ To introduce the concept of segmenting the leisure market, according to the different user group profiles
▶ To explore the practicalities of devising a suitable programme to cater for the needs of the user groups

Identifying user groups

Organisations must have a clear profile of the types of customers who are using their facility. The advantage of knowing who the customers are is that it helps in the planning of appropriate activities aimed at different user groups, e.g. young mothers, old age pensioners, etc. Equally, non-users and low participant groups can be identified.

We shall now explore the concept of user groups more specifically, by looking at demographic details (family, sex, age, housing), socio-economic groups, educational status, and minority groups.

Family

Sociologists often refer to the 'nuclear' family as a model for the modern day family. This typically comprises a mother, father and two children. The family life cycle takes this concept one step further, by dividing the family into different life cycle stages. It is useful for the leisure provider to be able to identify the stages of the family life cycle as each stage has specific needs and characteristics.

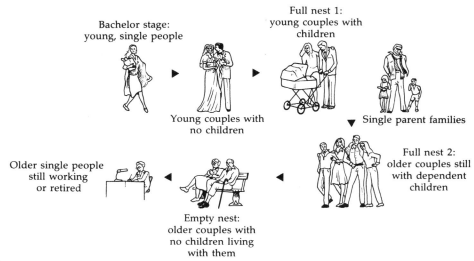

▲ *Figure 9.1   The family life cycle*

Look at the Table and complete the lifestyle characteristics for the remaining stages of the family life cycle. It will be helpful to base your assessments on commitments and priorities, disposable income, time available.

Life cycle stage	Lifestyle characteristics
Young singles	e.g. no major commitments, disposable income spent on self, large amount of leisure time
Young couples, no children	
Single parent, with children	
Young couples, with young children	
Older couples, older children at home	
Older couples, empty nest	
Older single people	

The pie charts in Figure 9.2 illustrate some of the family life cycle characteristics in Britain.

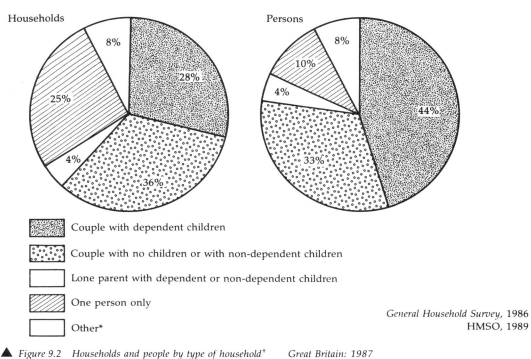

Households   Persons

General Household Survey, 1986
HMSO, 1989

Couple with dependent children

Couple with no children or with non-dependent children

Lone parent with dependent or non-dependent children

One person only

Other*

▲ *Figure 9.2   Households and people by type of household*[†]   *Great Britain: 1987*

*Other includes households containing two or more unrelated adults and those containing two or more families.
[†]Households categorised by the type of family they contain.
 In the lone parent and married couple households, other individuals who were not family members may also have been present.

1 Which category does your household fit into?
Is this category in the majority or minority? Why do you think this is so?

2 Comment on the percentage of households with one person only. What are the implications for this regarding leisure participation, and provision?

Sex

Are the users of leisure facilities mainly males or females? Is there a reasonable balance? Some activities may attract males more than females, or vice versa. The table below illustrates participation rates by men and women in leisure activities.

Table 9.1 Participation[1] in selected social and cultural activities: by sex, 1986[2]

Great Britain   *Percentages and numbers*

	All males[3]	All females[3]	All persons[3]
Percentage in each group engaging in each activity in the 4 weeks before interview			
Open air outings			
Seaside	6	8	7
Parks	3	4	4
Country	3	3	3
Entertainment, social and cultural activities			
Going out for a drink[4]	65	47	55
Going out for a meal	47	47	47
Dancing	9	12	11
Visiting historic buildings/ sites/towns	9	10	9
Going to the cinema	8	8	8
Going to the theatre/ opera/ballet	4	6	5
Going to fairs/amusement arcades	4	5	4
Going to museums/art galleries	4	4	4
Amateur music/drama	4	3	4
Home-based activities			
Listening to records/tapes[4]	69	65	67
Reading books[4]	52	64	59
Gardening[4]	47	39	43
House repairs/DIY[4]	54	27	39
Needlework/knitting/dressmaking[4]	3	48	27
Sample size (= 100%) (numbers)	8 891	10 318	19 209

1 Annual averages of participation of people aged 16 and over
2 Full-time students are covered separately
3 Includes armed forces, and persons who have worked. These are excluded from the analysis by socio-economic group
4 The high participation levels are partly attributable to the fact that these items were prompted (see Appendix, Part 10: General Household Survey)

Extract from table in *Social Trends 1990*
General Household Survey, 1986
HMSO, 1989

Age

Before considering the types of activities which attract different age groups, it is important to be aware of the age structure of society. This has undergone considerable changes in recent years.

Table 9.2 illustrates population changes from 1971–2031 (projected).

Table 9.2 Age distribution of the UK resident population: mid-year estimates and projections

Thousands

Persons all ages	1971	1976	1981	1986	1988 Base	1991	1996	2001	2011	2021	2031
	55 927	56 216	56 352	56 763	57 065	57 533	58 462	59 201	59 989	60 823	61 200
0–4	4 553	3 721	3 455	3 642	3 747	3 914	4 136	3 973	3 594	3 837	3 740
5–9	4 684	4 483	3 677	3 467	3 619	3 656	3 918	4 140	3 686	3 708	3 852
10–14	4 232	4 693	4 470	3 690	3 394	3 484	3 666	3 928	3 987	3 610	3 844
15–19	3 862	4 244	4 735	4 479	4 250	3 707	3 499	3 681	4 164	3 712	3 722
20–24	4 282	3 881	4 284	4 784	4 728	4 496	3 724	3 517	3 960	4 019	3 628
25–29	3 686	4 239	3 828	4 237	4 495	4 746	4 469	3 700	3 675	4 157	3 721
30–34	3 284	3 629	4 182	3 787	3 892	4 200	4 702	4 430	3 458	3 899	3 972
35–39	3 187	3 225	3 589	4 158	3 847	3 771	4 170	4 669	3 643	3 619	4 099
40–44	3 325	3 136	3 185	3 561	4 005	4 132	3 742	4 133	4 379	3 420	3 858
45–49	3 532	3 262	3 090	3 142	3 209	3 518	4 079	3 691	4 585	3 586	3 566
50–54	3 304	3 423	3 179	3 023	3 055	3 080	3 450	3 997	4 014	4 265	3 333
55–59	3 365	3 151	3 271	3 055	3 000	2 919	2 980	3 339	3 519	4 389	3 433
60–64	3 222	3 131	2 935	3 055	2 940	2 873	2 756	2 817	3 681	3 719	3 956
65–69	2 736	2 851	2 801	2 641	2 865	2 759	2 614	2 516	2 913	3 091	3 867
70–74	2 029	2 260	2 393	2 364	2 166	2 267	2 379	2 272	2 263	2 988	3 041
75–79	1 356	1 499	1 708	1 837	1 860	1 853	1 817	1 920	1 798	2 118	2 259
80–84	803	849	968	1 132	1 196	1 265	1 306	1 313	1 354	1 374	1 825
85 and over	485	538	602	709	796	894	1 056	1 166	1 315	1 313	1 484

From *General Household Survey* 1986
HMSO, 1989

Promoting participation

In the 1980s the Sports Council targeted specific promotion campaigns at certain age groups (see *Sport in the Community: the Next Ten Years,* a Sports Council publication). Two specific groups were identified:

- 13–24-year-olds
- 45–59-year-olds.

Each of these age groups were further sub-divided into the following:

13–24-year-olds

- School children
- College students
- Single young, the unencumbered, often with high incomes
- The unemployed
- Ethnic minorities
- Young marrieds with no children
- Low income young marrieds with children, under great financial pressure
- Higher income groups with children – concentrated in areas of population growth and jobs
- Single parents

45–59-year-olds

- High and low income people with children still at home
- One or both spouses unemployed, and single unemployed
- Early retired with golden handshakes or pensions
- Early retired because of sickness
- Early retired and re-engaged in work.

It was felt that it was important to target these age groups because 'they are at points of major change in life patterns, when new behaviours and attitudes are formed'. Consequently, any sports participation developed at these times 'is more likely to carry over into later periods of life'.

ACTIVITY

Consider the statement made by the Sport's Council about the age groups above.

1 Choose one of the sub-groups of the 45–59-year-olds and arrange an interview with someone who fits this category. (It will probably be someone known to you.)

2 Find out about how their life has changed compared to ten years ago, regarding their leisure time pursuits. Why have these changes taken place? Are they for the better or worse?

Educational status

Users with differing educational qualifications may be interested in pursuing different types of leisure pursuits. Figure 9.3 illustrates the number of visits to a library.

ACTIVITY

1 Comment on the trends illustrated in Figure 9.3. What conclusions can you draw?

2 What other activities do you think may be influenced by educational qualifications? Why?

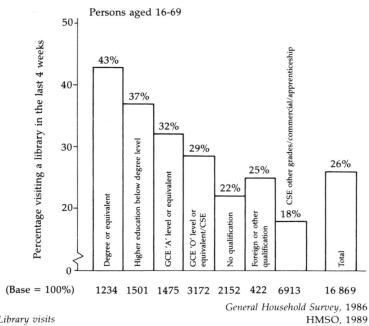

Persons aged 16-69

General Household Survey, 1986
HMSO, 1989

▲ *Figure 9.3   Library visits*

Socio-economic groups

According to the Registrar General, Britain has the following social classes:

A   The Monarchy, higher professional and landed gentry
B   Professional, managerial, e.g. doctors, dentists, solicitors
C1   Junior managerial, supervisory
C2   Skilled workers
D   Semi-skilled workers
E   Unskilled workers, pensioners on state pensions, widows and widowers and those on subsistence levels, e.g. the unemployed.

Table 9.3   Percentage of people seeing arts performances, visiting art galleries, museums and historic buildings in the 4 weeks before interview by socio-economic group

	Socio-economic group						
	Professional	Employers and managers	Intermediate and junior non-manual	Skilled manual and own account	Semi-skilled manual and personal service	Unskilled manual	Total
Arts and entertainments	Percentage participating in the 4 weeks before interview						
Films	15	11	12	8	8	5	11
Plays, pantomimes or musicals	13	10	10	4	4	3	7
Ballet or modern dance	1	1	1	1	ø	1	1
Operas or operettas	2	2	1	ø	ø	ø	1
Classical music	6	3	3	1	1	1	2
Jazz, blues, soul, reggae concerts or performances	2	2	2	1	1	0	2
Other music shows, concerts or performances	9	7	8	7	6	5	7
Galleries and historic buildings							
Art galleries or museums	15	11	11	6	5	4	8
Stately homes, castles, cathedrals or other historic buildings	14	11	10	6	5	4	8
Base = 100%	*705*	*2 465*	*6 012*	*4 051*	*3 830*	*1 265*	*19 529*

From *General Household Survey* 1987
HMSO, 1989

Socio-economic groups are based on the occupation of the head of the household. There is increasing criticism about the use of socio-economic groups as an accurate means of categorising society nowadays because, in many ways, there is evidence that classes are merging and 'head of the household' is no longer a useful term in most cases. However, there is still evidence that socio-economic groups have a significant influence on the way leisure time is used.

/ACTIVITY/

Refer to Table 9.3, page 93.

1 Summarise the participation trends by socio-economic group for each activity.

2 Suggest reasons for your results.

Because of the ambiguity of dividing people into classes, it is increasingly common to group people into housing types, based on the assumption that people with similar characteristics, lifestyles, etc. live in similar types of housing. ACORN is one such classification of residential neighbourhoods, consisting of the following eleven categories:

A   **Agricultural areas**

B   **Modern family housing, higher incomes**

C   **Older housing of intermediate status**

D   **Poor quality older terraced housing**

E   **Better-off council estates**

F   **Less well-off council estates**

G   **Poorest council estates**

H   **Multi-racial areas**

I   **High status non-family areas**

J   **Affluent suburban housing**

K   **Better-off retirement areas**

▲ *Figure 9.4   Acorn table © CACI Ltd.*

/ACTIVITY/

Choose one of the housing groups from the list above, and carry out a mini survey in your chosen area to test out the theory that 'People with similar lifestyles live in similar types of housing'. Remember that you are particularly concerned with their leisure lifestyles.

Ethnic minorities

Britain is a multi-cultural society, and different sub-cultures may have different needs which have to be catered for. In some areas, ethnic minorities may comprise a large group and may organise activities themselves. However there may be groups of this nature in the vicinity whose needs are not being met. For example, there may be no provision for Afro-Caribbean dancing, Irish National dancing, etc.

▲ *Two different types of housing. The house you live in can have a direct effect on your leisure activities*
▼

General minority groups and sport participation

They can be divided into two groups: those who are considered low participant in sporting activities and those who are non-participants. Let us first consider the low participant groups. The Sports Council has identified these as being:

a) Those newly moved to an area, especially from overseas
b) The unemployed
c) Older women
d) Over 45s generally
e) The disabled, especially the mentally disabled.

Non-participants comprise the following:

a) Housewives
b) Semi and unskilled workers
c) Non car-owners
d) Lower income groups.

Disabled users of centres

People in this category may be either mentally or physically disabled, or both. The British Disabled Sports Foundation has further categorised disabled people into those who are physically mobile (S1), and those who are confined to a wheelchair (W1). There are then further sub-divisions in each of these groups, so that differing degrees of mobility are classified. This process of categorisation enables disabled competitors to be divided as fairly as possible in competitive activities.

However, the majority of disabled people participate in sport and leisure for social reasons. Social interaction increases confidence – a quality which many disabled people lack. Disabled people have been identified as a low participant group in sport generally, and it needs to be recognised that they have many psychological and sometimes physical barriers to overcome. Many disabled users may not be economically active; they will have less disposable income to spend on leisure, but may be able to participate in off-peak periods.

A significant factor which encourages participation by physically disabled users is the design of centres. For example, ramps, lifts and special toilets are necessary for wheelchairs. Doorways need to be wide enough for wheelchair access, and notice boards should ideally be at a conveniently lower height.

Physically disabled users may need a helper to come with them to the leisure activity, and may be restricted to the times when special transport can be laid on.

PHAB clubs

PHAB (Physically Handicapped and Able Bodied) clubs are run locally for able-bodied and disabled people together. They generally meet once a week and there are special outings to the theatre, etc. Some outdoor centres supply specially adapted sailing boats and canoes, so that groups of this nature can enjoy outdoor activities.

Programming

Now that we have considered the characteristics and needs of user groups, the next step is to understand the factors involved in programming leisure activities.

Regardless of whether the facility is a sports hall, a theatre, a concert hall, or a local community centre, careful programming of activities which cater for the needs of the user groups is vital to the success of the organisation. Sometimes, the ideal programme may not be feasible in terms of costs and as a result certain user groups may not be catered for. In the commercial sector programming must be profitable; in the public sector, where some subsidies are available, there is more scope to cater for the needs of the minority groups.

Club versus individual usage

Sometimes there may be competition between different user groups for more time to be given to them. This dilemma is often faced by leisure centre managers, where clubs (e.g. hockey, badminton) may be demanding more booking time for club usage of facilities. The manager needs to make sure that there is sufficient space on the programme for casual users to book sports hall space. This may be more financially risky, since a regular club booking is more financially secure than leaving space empty in the hope that someone will book it!

Peak versus off-peak

Most leisure facilities have peak periods, when demand outstrips supply (often during the evenings and at weekends), and off-peak times (often during the day) when the opposite is true. Programming for off-peak periods can be problematic. However, there are certain user groups who have leisure time during the day – housewives, shift workers, and senior citizens, for example. Imaginative programming together with price concessions, can increase usage of any facility and therefore contribute to running costs, or even profitability.

Let us look at some mini case studies, to illustrate the various factors involved in programming.

Focus on the YMCA

This national voluntary organisation is non-profit-making and has a commitment to health and fitness. A programme of exercise to music is offered during the evenings, catering for beginners to advanced. When planning the programme the following points have to be considered:

- A break-even point has to be calculated. The break-even point is where the costs of the enterprise are balanced out by the income received.
- Tutors are recruited on a part-time basis – they mostly have full-time jobs and are only available in the evenings.
- There needs to be a reserve pool of tutors willing to fill in when someone is absent.
- Classes cannot really be progressive as there is a drop-in system, where people pay as they come. No prior commitment to a particular class is necessary.
- The programme should be balanced, providing for the needs of people at various levels of fitness.
- Reasonable levels of charges must be maintained in keeping with the philosophy of the YMCA.
- A maximum number, for example, 25 is imposed for any class depending on room size; any more would be uncomfortable, and would be a health risk.

Here is a sample of a typical programme that is offered:

Monday	**Tuesday**
6–7 Aerobics for beginners	6–7 Fun aerobics
7–8 Intermediate aerobics	7–8 Aerobics general
8–9 Advanced aerobics	8–9 Jazz aerobics

/ **ACTIVITY** /

1 Complete the programme for Wednesday, Thursday and Friday, from 6–9 pm, bearing in mind the user groups you are aiming to attract. The aim is to achieve a balanced programme!

2 Compare the programming policy of the YMCA to that of a commercial company. How far are the policy differences of the two organisations reflected in the programme content and the conditions under which it runs?

3 Assume that the total cost of room hire and tutor salary per exercise class is £16 per hour.
   Work out the minimum number of people required for each class in order to break even at the following price rates:
   a) £2 per class
   b) £2.50 per class
   c) £3.00 per class.

4 What gross profit would be made if there were a maximum number of 25 participants at each class? Work out the profit for each of the price charges: £2, £2.50 and £3.00, respectively.

Focus on the Old Agricultural Hall

The Old Agricultural Hall is a public sector concert hall which can also be used for exhibitions and films. When planning the programme the following points have to be considered:

- As a public sector facility it aims to serve the needs of the whole community.
- Rock and pop concerts generally attract capacity audiences, and are therefore profitable.

- As many performances are for only one or two nights, there needs to be an efficient turn-around system by the technicians (taking down lighting, setting up equipment, etc.) to get the hall ready for the next event.
- Exhibitions and conferences need to be included as they mainly use off-peak periods in the day.
- Minority entertainment such as classical music and folk music usually has to be subsidised.
- There are seasonal peaks and troughs; in January, for example, when it is difficult to contract groups, the hall can be used as a cinema. This tends to be profit-making.
- The size of the hall will determine which entertainers are prepared to perform there, i.e. if it is too small, perhaps more famous groups will not be prepared to perform. Dance companies may have particular problems if the stage is not big enough.

Here is a sample of a programme for the Old Agricultural Hall:

Monday	The Supremes
Tuesday	The Dubliners
Wednesday	Regional Symphony Orchestra
Thursday	Simply Red
Friday	Contemporary Dance Company
Saturday	Finals of Local Rock Group Competition
Sunday	

/ACTIVITY/

1 Analyse the programme and state which user groups each event aims to attract. Give detailed profiles of each.

2 Obtain a programme from a similar venue near you and write a short analysis, bearing in mind the points outlined in the case study.

Focus on Grafham Water

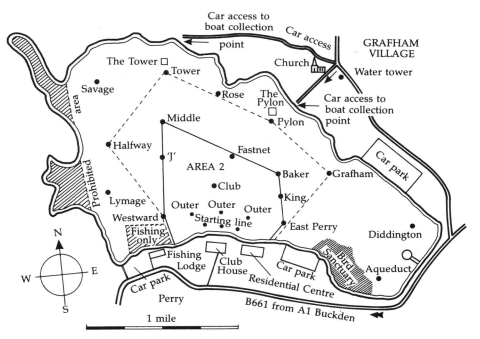

▲ *Figure 9.5 Plan of Grafham Warer*

Grafham Water is an inland reservoir; its primary industry is supplying water for domestic and industrial purposes. It is part of a public limited company. A secondary function of the reservoir is to provide water sports facilities such as sailing, windsurfing, canoeing and fishing. The reservoir has a thriving sailing and windsurfing clubhouse, as well as a residential centre operated by the local Education Authority. There is also a fishing lodge and nature reserve.

The residential centre provides a programme of watersports courses for schools and institutions within the country, as well as general courses for the public. In addition, it is a centre for environmental studies, and there are a number of non-water sports courses offered, such as painting and drawing, woodcarving, creative writing, etc.

When devising a programme for the Centre, the following factors have to be considered:

- The Centre operates seasonally from April to October.
- As an educational establishment, there is an emphasis on teaching people new skills safely.
- Course members resident in the county are charged reduced rates – school and youth groups are charged a group rate.
- Courses are offered on a midweek basis, Monday to Friday, or weekends.
- The programme needs to cater for a variety of levels, with a greater emphasis on beginners' courses.
- There are 40 residential places available, but non-residents are welcome and pay reduced fees.

Here is a sample of a typical programme for the centre:

Friday–Sunday: Beginners' sailing, Advanced sailing, Beginners' windsurfing, Fly-fishing
Monday–Thursday: Mixed activities – school group
Friday–Sunday: Creative writing course (winter/spring)

ACTIVITY

1 Devise a suitable programme for the school group mixed activity course. Plan your activities on a half-day basis.

2 Produce a publicity leaflet for the programme you have devised, including a sample programme, aims of the course, details of facilities, and any other information which you feel is relevant.

Summary

▶ It is possible to segment user groups in various ways so that a profile of current and non-users can be built up.
▶ It is important to bear in mind social trends, such as the age structure, where population trends in the 1990s indicate a growing number of middle-aged and older people.
▶ Programming activities for user groups must be undertaken with a clear profile of the needs of the user groups concerned. There may be many external factors which influence the structure of the programme, and these factors have to be fully realised before any planning takes place.
▶ It is important to recognise that customers should not be considered en masse, as the 'general public', but as separate user groups, each having different needs.
▶ Remember that different user groups have different participation rates for different activities.

10 *The leisure pound*

Aims

▶ To define what is meant by disposable income
▶ To identify factors which influence the amount of disposable income people have
▶ To explain the concepts of market share and diversification

Disposable income

Disposable income refers to the amount of money individuals have available after compulsory deductions (e.g. national insurance, tax) and voluntary deductions (pension funds, union subscriptions, Save As You Earn schemes, etc.) from their income have been met. What remains is known as **net disposable income**, and from this an individual has to pay rent or a mortgage, indirect taxes and charges, e.g. the community charge (see Chapter 6), household bills, food, etc. After essential expenditure has been made, the remaining disposable income may be spent on leisure pursuits.

Figure 10.1 shows the predicted changes in real personal disposable income into the 1990s. It indicates a predicted fall in the growth of disposable income in 1990. The rapid proliferation of credit products and ease of access to products has led to increased access to spending in recent years. People have been spending more than they earn, so that consumer indebtedness has risen and savings have fallen. Added to this there has been a rise in owner-occupation so that increases in the mortgage rate from the late 1980s has resulted in less personal disposable income.

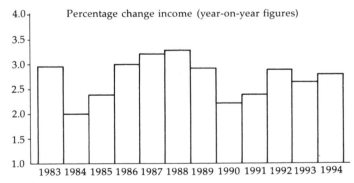

From *Leisure Management*, Vol. 9, No. 5, 1989

▲ *Figure 10.1   Changes in disposable income*

Changes in real disposable income

It is important to remember that external factors such as higher mortgages, inflation, high interest rates or increased direct taxes will affect the amount of disposable income available to be spent on leisure pursuits. In addition, indirect taxation on products (VAT – currently running at 15 per cent) increases prices so that the higher the VAT, the less disposable income people have.

Affluence

Although the outlook in real terms looks gloomy, consumers will continue to grow more affluent into the 1990s. There is a minimum level of affluence required before leisure activities become a realistic option. For the majority of people this minimum level has been reached. This is partly due to higher incomes and expenditure on food as a share of total consumer spending has been declining for a number of years.

Leisure organisations have to compete to win their share of the leisure pound in your pocket, since it is only after basic needs have been fulfilled that consumers are likely to indulge in the purchase of leisure goods and services. Figure 10.2 illustrates the leisure industry's share of consumer spending for 1988.

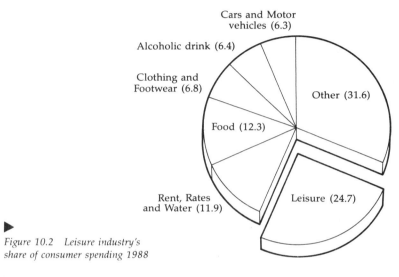

Figure 10.2   Leisure industry's share of consumer spending 1988

From *Leisure Management*, Vol. 9, No. 5, 1989

Table 10.1   UK household expenditure on selected leisure items: by household income, 1986

United Kingdom

£ and percentages

	Gross normal weekly income of household						
	Up to £100	*Over £100, up to £150*	*Over £150, up to £200*	*Over £200, up to £250*	*Over £250, up to £300*	*Over £300*	*All house-holds*
Average weekly household expenditure on (£):							
Alcoholic drink consumed away from home	1.67	3.64	5.23	6.23	7.73	10.63	5.93
Meals consumed out[1]	1.03	2.00	3.00	3.66	4.65	9.43	4.38
Books, newspapers, magazines, etc.	1.46	2.13	2.53	2.75	3.10	4.16	2.73
Television, radio and musical instruments	2.09	3.05	4.45	5.79	6.39	7.62	4.85
Purchase of materials for home repairs, etc.	0.84	2.01	2.03	2.96	3.63	6.00	3.08
Holidays	0.65	1.75	3.24	4.30	5.26	12.95	5.39
Hobbies	0.03	0.03	0.06	0.07	0.06	0.11	0.06
Cinema admissions	0.03	0.04	0.08	0.09	0.11	0.20	0.10
Dance admissions	0.03	0.06	0.07	0.12	0.18	0.24	0.12
Theatre, concert, etc, admissions	0.05	0.17	0.18	0.26	0.25	0.64	0.29
Subscription and admission charges to participant sports	0.08	0.36	0.38	0.68	0.86	1.59	0.71
Football match admissions	0.01	0.07	0.03	0.13	0.10	0.14	0.08
Admissions to other spectator sports	0.02	0.01	0.02	0.03	0.05	0.07	0.04
Sports goods (excluding clothes)	0.09	0.14	0.17	0.42	0.28	0.83	0.37
Other entertainment	0.10	0.19	0.31	0.33	0.49	0.86	0.41
Total weekly expenditure on above	8.18	15.64	21.76	27.83	33.15	55.46	28.54
Expenditure on above items as a percentage of total household expenditure	11.3	12.6	13.7	15.7	16.2	18.3	16.0

[1]Eaten on the premises, excluding state school meals and workplace meals.   Central Statistical Office, from *Family Expenditure Survey* 1989

┌─/ACTIVITY/───┐

1 Refer to Figure 10.1, page 101. How are external factors currently affecting the
   level of personal disposable income? Why?

2 Calculate your own disposable income for a week and draw a bar chart to
   illustrate your expenditure on the leisure activities which you pursue.
└──┘

Market share

To help understand this concept, imagine a round cake, cut into slices, with each slice representing a 'share' of the market. Not all slices are of the same thickness: this is also true of market shares – some are greater than others. If you refer once again to Figure 10.2 it will be apparent that certain leisure organisations have a far greater share of the market than others. Consider Table 10.1 and then read the following before attempting the activity on page 104.

Pubs and breweries

People appear to spend most money on alcohol consumed away from home, which indicates that breweries and pubs have the largest market shares.

Holidays

Expenditure on holidays closely follows the percentage spent on alcohol. This would then indicate that tour operators, the main providers of holidays, should be doing well. However, tourism is a very volatile market. The very hot summers of 1976, 1989 and 1990 encouraged people to stay at home, rather than go abroad, and as domestic holidays are traditionally booked independently, tour operators suffered a considerable loss of sales so that their share of the market declined. Another continuing threat to their share of the market is the growing desire of British tourists to travel independently, hence threatening the package holiday market. In future tour operators will have to fight harder to sustain their market shares.

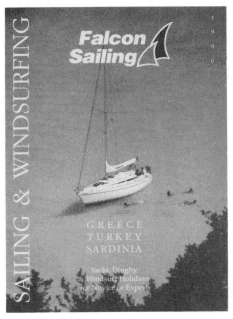

◀ Special interest holidays are growing in popularity. They can cover a variety of interests, e.g. sailing, wildlife watching, golfing, rambling, water sports and keeping fit

DIY

The DIY market which increased in the 1980s is, however, dependent on the housing market. In 1989 the stagnant housing market, which came about as a result of high interest rates, had a knock-on effect on the DIY market. As fewer people are able to buy and sell houses, the demand for DIY products generally declines. Conversely, in a buoyant housing market, the DIY market share increases.

Gardening

Hobbies such as gardening have always been popular, with the result that garden centres are enjoying a growing commercial success.

Cinema

The decline in cinema attendances resulted when television first appeared in the 1950s, and suffered again when the home video market expanded. In the late 1980s cinema audiences showed signs of increasing, perhaps because of the better quality viewing on the big screen, improved sound equipment, coupled with the 'blockbuster' films which appeal to a broad market.

/ ACTIVITY /

Look at Table 10.1, page 102. What is the connection between income and expenditure on leisure items? Analyse each income category.

Market share size

Market share size is of particular interest to commercial leisure organisations, who continuously battle to sustain their share, or, more importantly, to increase it. Business organisations grow in size or take over and merge with other firms, specifically to gain larger market shares for their products or services. An example of this is Thomson Holidays' take over of the tour operator Horizon.

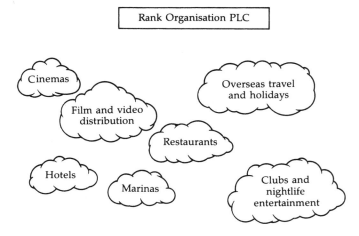

▲ *Figure 10.3 Rank PLC interests*

Sometimes the aim is not just to ensure larger market shares for one product or service, but to **diversify**, e.g. by breaking into new and different markets. Cigarette companies such as Peter Stuyvesant, for example, may buy into the leisure industry. The idea is to spread their risk and not put all their eggs into one basket. Another example of diversification is the Rank Organisation PLC which has interests in the cinema and film industries in addition to restaurants, overseas travel, holidays, hotels and marinas. The group also manufactures photocopiers (Rank Xerox), scientific instruments, optical products, TV broadcast equipment, TV studios and theatre lighting.

Integration

Business organisations can integrate **horizontally** or **vertically**. An example of horizontal integration would be a private leisure centre taking over another; the two organisations are at the same level in the **chain of distribution**. If a brewery took over a chain of restaurants or hotels this would be an example of vertical integration, as the organisations are at different levels in the distribution chain (see Figure 10.4).

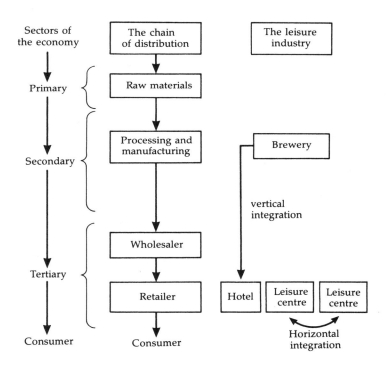

▲ *Figure 10.4   The chain of distribution*

Summary

▶ The success of many leisure organisations is linked to external factors in the economy. The amount of disposable income people have left to spend on leisure is dependent on factors such as mortgage rates, taxes, inflation, etc.
▶ Certain sections of the leisure industry have larger shares of the total market than others.
▶ In order to increase market share size companies may diversify into new markets, merge or take over other companies at the same or different levels of the distribution chain.

USER SURVEY

Choose one of the following user age groups:
- 50+ males and females
- disabled
- 13–24 females
- 13–24 males
- 45–59 males and females.

1 Carry out a survey to find out how they spend their disposable income.

2 Write an informal report about your findings, and identify which local leisure organisations benefit from their leisure pound.

Aims

▶ To illustrate the role of the manager in a leisure organisation
▶ To illustrate the role of operational staff in leisure organisations
▶ To underline the importance of motivation and attitudes
▶ To show the career structures in the leisure industry

Management styles

Modern leisure management demands the same business skills and training that managers in other industries require. Whether the organisation is in the public sector, private sector or is a voluntary group, there will be a need to plan, implement, monitor, initiate, control, lead and appraise.

Because leisure is a very 'people-centred' industry, it is vital that the manager is able to motivate staff, who are responsible for delivering the leisure product.

Since the 1950s there has been a tendency to adopt a more flexible approach to management, as opposed to rigid structuring. The work of a well-known psychologist, David Maslow, encouraged the belief that people should be able to express themselves in work and leisure. He saw individuals as having certain needs which they are constantly striving to fulfil. The satisfaction that derives from achieving each level of need, shown within a hierarchical structure (Figure 11.1), leads to improved work and work relationships. In an affluent society, most physical and social needs have been satisfied. Social and ego needs dominate. As each goal is achieved, so the next is sought.

▶

Figure 11.1   Maslow's Theory of Self-Actualisation

If needs are unsatisfied, the results can be frustration, deterioration in work performance, neurosis, and ulcers. In 1959 another behaviourist, Frederick Herzberg, added to Maslow's work by stressing the importance of factors such as organisational policy and rules, management style and controls, retirement and sickness policies and pay and recognition of status.

Extrinsic motivation

This is the motivation a person obtains external to the job itself, e.g. good salary, and perks such as company car and use of the social club.

Intrinsic motivation

This applies to the satisfaction a person derives from doing the actual job itself – some people call this **job satisfaction**. An actor can derive great satisfaction from entertaining the public, for example.

How do you motivate staff?

- Setting targets
- Incentives such as bonuses, pay rises, profit sharing, fringe benefits, shares in company
- Promotion prospects.

What is leadership?

Management cannot be separated from leadership. Leaders have personal traits such as initiative, courage and intelligence. Modern managers have to ask themselves what the most appropriate leadership style is in any given situation.

/ **ACTIVITY** /

1 Devise a questionnaire to find out how people working in the local leisure industry are motivated and de-motivated.

2 Carry out a mini survey and give feedback on your findings to the rest of the group.

Focus on the Old Corn Exchange

A day in the life of a manager . . .
Extract from Bob Black's diary entry on Thursday 16 June

9 a.m.	Appointment John Downing, City Hall (End of Year Accounts)
1 p.m.	Lunch Red Lion (speak to Colin/Sam – security for tonight)
2.15 p.m.	Check Fenwicken Caterers (at Corn Exchange) Programme for July (Can they cater for private party on the 4 July, 150 people?)
3.00 p.m.	Interviews for part-time staff (Box Office) (Refer Rosie – has she completed ticket sales sheet for May?)
4.30 p.m.	Desmond Cartwright, *Evening News* Reporter, publicity for European Conference, 14 August (my office – with Rosie)
7.30–10.30 p.m.	Heaven Sent gig – young audience (check with Colin in Technical – OK?)

Inside the large rectangular yellow brick building is a booking hall (or foyer), bar, café, main auditorium with stage, dressing rooms, and various ante-rooms back stage. On the upper levels there are some smaller gallery rooms which are ideal for exhibitions and have a view of the main auditorium, another bar, the toilets and a large square room, ideal for private functions, away from the main hall. Two or more events could be held at the same time.

The Old Corn Exchange is a renovated building in the centre of a large town. Originally it was built to assist the trading of agricultural produce for local farmers, but recently it has been refurbished as an entertainment and concert venue by the local council. It now caters for a

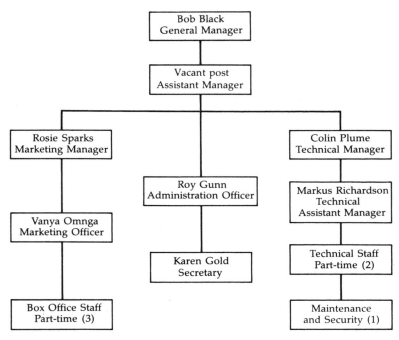

▲ *Figure 11.2* *The Old Corn Exchange organisation chart*

spectrum of different users; students attend concerts there, at other times there are fashion shows, tea dances, classical concerts, film shows, conferences, art exhibitions, discos, ballroom evenings and so on, ensuring that business people, the elderly, families and young professionals should all find something there of interest to them.

It is to the credit of the General Manager of this organisation, Bob Black, that the organisation has been so successful for the past six months. When he transferred to this job, from the Amenities Department in a London Borough, he was apprehensive of the pressures of the new job. Bob is single and 35 years old, with a girlfriend in London, and he wondered how she would feel as the new job required shift work, unsocial hours and dedication to problem solving. Luckily, although the job has proved to be as demanding as he envisaged, his girlfriend has decided to re-locate to work for an accountancy firm in the same town.

The team of people Bob is responsible for are lively and outgoing. Often they have the bright ideas for the entertainment that is provided. Once a month there is a full staff meeting: everyone is expected to attend to give a progress report on their own area of responsibility, and to hear the update on planning for the future. Bob is pleased that these meetings seem to be successful and when we talked to the part-time box office staff, even they were genuinely interested in the organisation's progress. They believe they are much more involved in the organisation than they were before Bob took over. However, they also feel that the team approach only works because there are so few employees in the organisation.

Vanya, the Marketing Officer, said: 'We're all of a similar age here (in fact Bob is the eldest at 35!) and it seems we all have quite similar interests so we get on well together. This means that during working hours there are few problems with arguments about who should be doing what and the bosses are quite approachable.'

Her boss, Rosie, commented: 'When Bob joined we were a much more traditional public sector organisation. Now we react much more to suggestions from the customers and clients. We provide a service, yet in most cases make a profit on events. Now the café is run by a firm of outside caterers [Fenwicken Caterers] so we don't have that to worry about and we concern ourselves really with providing what the public want in the form of entertainment'.

Rosie told us that she has a degree in business studies from a polytechnic and is able to put some of her theoretical knowledge into practice using market research techniques to find out

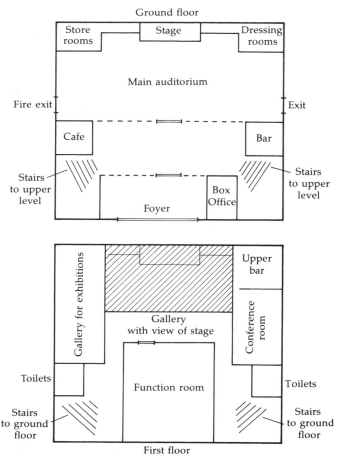

▲ *Figure 11.3   Plan of the Old Corn Exchange*

exactly what different users want. Bob is keen to support her in this project provided that she keeps him informed of progress.

On the technical side, Colin has this to say: 'Yes, Bob's a great bloke. It's really good to have someone who can understand some of the electrical problems we have to deal with and doesn't hide in the office all the time. He's very approachable and what I really appreciate is the way he lets me get on with my job without hassling me, yet is there when I have a really difficult time. It's not that he lends a hand, but he gives moral support and suggests ways to deal with situations. He's often here at midnight'.

At present the post of Assistant Manager is vacant, but Bob has advertised the job and hopes to hold interviews by the end of the month. He envisages including both the Technical Manager, Colin, and the Marketing Manager, Rosie, in the job interviews, in order that they can give their opinions on interviewees.

Specification for job of Old Corn Exchange General Manager (Bob Black's job)
1 Responsible for finance and cash flow of the organisation. To liaise with the local authority with regard to yearly budgets and income and expenditure.
2 Overall responsibility for marketing, box office ticket sales and bar, within guidelines set by local authority. Specific delegation of tasks to Marketing Manager.
3 Organisation of catering tender for café and constant monitoring of this on a six-monthly basis.
4 Responsible for the smooth running of technical operations. Specific delegation of tasks to Technical Manager.

5 Overall responsibility for security and maintenance of premises. Delegation of tasks to security and maintenance person via the Technical Manager.

6 Sole responsibility for recruitment and selection of staff within the organisation.

7 Allowed to appoint an assistant manager in order to facilitate the operation of the organisation.

8 The General Manager, with the help of an assistant, is expected to:

   a) Plan the overall strategy for the organisation and programme of activities, in conjunction with the local authority.

   b) Organise the staff to accept responsibility for parts of this strategy.

   c) Co-ordinate the smooth running of the organisation.

   d) Motivate staff in order to achieve the provision of a service for the public and, if possible, a trading surplus or profit.

ACTIVITY

Read through the Old Corn Exchange case study and complete the following tasks:

1 What kind of qualities do you think Bob Black has? In particular, focus on his personal characteristics and make a list of the ones which enable him to be a successful manager.

2 From the comments the staff make about him, how capable is he at his job? How would you rate him as a boss and how could he improve his skills?

3 What kind of academic qualifications do you think are necessary for all aspects of this kind of work? You may refer to other parts of this chapter or even the *Handbook of Tourism and Leisure* (a Hobson's Directory) in order to answer this question.

4 Draw up a job specification for the post of Assistant Manager at the Old Corn Exchange. Complete a seperate list of the personal characteristics and skills you think the person should possess. What kind of academic qualifications do you think are necessary?

The role of the manager

A manager should possess leadership qualities, but this does not mean strictly imposing his or her own views and ideas to deal with different situations. Each situation that occurs in the organisation may require a different approach; sometimes a strong lead is required, at other times a more democratic process may be preferred. If staff feel they have been consulted over situations that occur and have given their opinions, they feel more involved in the decision-making process and more interested in the organisation. Most importantly the manager must be a good communicator, able to talk and relate to people who have different levels of authority and hold different opinions. This is necessary in order to transmit messages successfully and to maintain good working relationships.

How a manager is expected to deal with a problem

1 Tells
2 Sells
3 Consults
4 Shares
5 Delegates.

Example

The problem: Head Office have decided that, in future, training courses for staff involved in a multinational leisure centre chain will be restricted. The manager must advise the 30 branch staff; 20 of the staff have been booked to attend training sessions in Holland and it looks likely that these will be cancelled. All the staff are going to be disappointed, and morale is likely to fall.

Solving the problem:

Step 1: Tells   Staff must be told of the new Head Office ruling regarding the cutbacks in training. A full staff meeting must be booked at the earliest opportunity.

Step 2: Sells   At the meeting the staff have to be 'sold' the idea: the reasons why Head Office have had to cut back training programmes must be given.

Step 3: Consults   The manager now decides to launch an alternative scheme as he or she believes that morale in the organisation will fall too low. The manager may ask for suggestions from the staff on how they think that the organisation could find the money for future training for staff. The manager may even ask what alternatives the staff may have to the training schemes in Holland.

Step 4: Shares   Another staff meeting is called in order that everyone involved knows what alternative suggestions have been made. Any other comments by Head Office must be passed on.

Step 5: Delegates   The staff are asked to vote on the suggestions made by the branch. A person or department is advised to draw up detailed plans of the new proposed training scheme, or funding for training, to submit to Head Office.

This, of course, is only one way to solve the problem. If you were in charge of the organisation you might have other ideas on how to solve it. There are no clear cut solutions to many of the problems encountered in managing an organisation, but a clear head and empathy with the staff (i.e. 'walking around in their shoes') does provide a good strategy for practical solutions.

A good manager will combine an ability to plan ahead and organise time effectively with the role of co-ordinating and motivating staff. It is no longer enough to sit behind an office door and issue orders to subordinates. The staff of an organisation are a resource and, as such, must believe they are involved in an organisation and appreciated for their skills.

ACTIVITY

Place yourself in the role of a manager of a leisure organisation and, with the aid of the step-by-step approach to a problem, jot down how you would solve the following situations with the assistance of your staff;

1   An overnight break-in at the premises; £10 000 of equipment and sports clothing has been stolen. Police suspect it may be an 'inside job' but you only have a staff of 15 and believe all are trustworthy. Write down the five steps and decide how you would plan how to deal with this situation.

2   The profits of your organisation have fallen from £200 000 a year to only £50 000. There is no single cause but increased labour costs, increased rent and high business rates are the major contributors. You must advise staff that there will be redundancies.

3   The target set for membership of your organisation has been increased by 50 per cent by your Head Office. You are expected to reach this target at the end of a twelve-month period. If you do not your job is 'on the line' and you will not get the further promotion you seek. What do you do?

Communication

This is important to the manager both for the maintenance of personal relationships and for the efficient transmission of messages.

Effective communications are maintained through:

- Regular staff meetings, where the manager consults and negotiates
- Staff and customer notice-boards
- Staff magazine
- Staff appraisal meetings
- Good telephone techniques
- Customer complaints/suggestion box
- Written communication such as memos, reports
- Non-verbal communication (body-language).

Management planning

The manager has four major resources – people, equipment, money and time. All these elements need to be taken into consideration when planning ahead. Plans may be long-term, such as enlarging the gym facilities, or short term, such as the planning of the weekly staff shift rota. Medium term plans may involve offering a new product such as 'fitness classes for the unfit'. Whatever the nature of the plan, however, the manager must carefully consider the resources available. Let us consider each one individually.

People

The manager needs to look at the skills of all members of the staff and appraise their strengths and weaknesses carefully. There is no point in trying to implement a plan if the human resources are not available. For instance, there is little point in planning a 'ladies only morning' with crèche facilities, run on a voluntary basis, if the mothers are not willing to volunteer to take a turn at looking after the children. Without the mothers' commitment, the plan is doomed to failure.

Equipment

The leisure manager needs to ensure that the right equipment is available for the activity. For example, if a weight training room is offered as a facility for non-body builders, there must be a sufficient number of lighter free weights available, heavier weights should not be supplied. It is vital that the equipment is maintained regularly, otherwise the manager may be accused of negligence. On the administrative side, the manager has to ensure that equipment, such as closed circuit TV, computerised booking systems, etc. is utilised to aid staff efficiency.

Money

It is important to consider the money available to carry out any plans. This must be carefully measured against the money required. If the plan is to run a two-day squash coaching course, the manager must take into consideration the cost of the courts, use of equipment and the coaching fees, which must be met in order to break even.

Time

Managers need to be methodical and disciplined in their approach to time planning. It is useful to break up the day into half hour slots and analyse the use of time. If a manager is spending time on unnecessary tasks, then it may be because he or she is badly organised or does not delegate to subordinates enough. If the manager has an 'open door' policy it may be necessary to have an appointment system for less urgent staff problems. There is an old adage that time means money, and wise managers need to constantly appraise their use (or misuse) of time.

/ACTIVITY/

1 Conduct your own time management plan over the period of a week by recording everything you do during the working day.

2 Analyse how you could have used the time more effectively. For example, how often were you distracted from tasks? What was the cause of this?

Career structure in the leisure industry

Due to the diverse nature of the leisure industry there is no general clear-cut career structure. It is fairly open industry in terms of promotion prospects and it is still possible to 'work up' from a basic job into a management position.

What basic jobs are there, and how can I find out about them?

At a basic level, you may start out as a trainee recreation assistant, gym instructor, pool attendant, or a general assistant in a theatre or entertainments complex.

Basic level jobs are often advertised in the local newspapers. It may be worthwhile writing to the local sports or leisure centre, or other organisation to express your interest in working in the industry, so that if a position does become vacant, your name will be on file. Although you may not need any specific qualifications at this level, a 'cheerful outgoing personality' and an 'enthusiasm for working with people', together with smart appearance are often mentioned as being 'desirable' qualities by employers.

What duties would you be expected to do?

Below is a job description for a Recreation Assistant in a leisure centre. It may surprise you that undertaking cleaning duties and maintaining equipment are important tasks which you must be prepared to carry out. In addition, you will need to be willing to work a regular shift system.

What qualifications can I get which will enhance my career prospects?

Many colleges of further education run courses which you may start at 16 years old. Vocational qualifications include The City and Guilds Recreation and Leisure Studies

---

Job description:
Recreation Assistant

Responsible to
The Sports Hall Management through the Recreation Co-ordinators.

Liaison
With all other Recreation Assistants, Receptionists, Assistant Manager/Maintenance and his staff.

Duties and responsibilities
1 To set up for events all equipment attached to the Sports Hall prior to events and activities.
2 To break down and store all equipment after the above events.
3 To ensure that all equipment attached to the Sports Hall is of a satisfactory condition with regard to security, safety and appearance.
4 To ensure that all equipment is maintained and in good repair.
5 To ensure that all equipment is stored and racked into the agreed areas of storage and the stock control system adhered to.
6 To teach and coach classes, groups and individuals at the Sports Centre, as agreed with the management team.
7 To fit into a 'loose' shift system to ensure adequate supervision of the casual programme, coaching courses and the 'one off' events, as required by the management team.
8 To police the building in all areas and see that the high standard of cleanliness and behaviour is maintained at all times.
9 To be adequately qualified in First Aid, to render same when necessary to do so.
10 To maintain the on-going standard of cleaning in all sports activity areas of the Sports Centre.
11 To check regularly all fire doors and fire exits to ensure that these are kept clear for access.
12 To report and record any damage to equipment or the fabric of the building.
13 To take responsibility for such specialities as designated by the Recreation Co-ordinators.
14 To train for Duty Manager role and occasionally experience such role, both under supervision and unsupervised.
15 To assist the Duty Manager in the smooth running of the building by affording cover for Bar, Café, Reception, etc. in cases of emergency.
16 To actively participate in the Duty Officer's rotas and to undertake such responsibilities as are included in the Duty Officer duties.
17 It is recognised that the post of Recreation Assistant does not make a fixed working week practicable and this is reflected in the salary level. Enhanced payments will continue to be paid for unsociable hours worked with the prior agreement of the Manager.

courses, which are relevant to swimming pool and leisure centre staff. Following on from this, there is a NEBSS (National Education Board for Supervisory Skills) Certificate with a Leisure specialism, suitable for employees aspiring to supervisor level.

Alternatively, if you are unsure about which sector of the industry you wish to go into, you could follow a BTEC (Business and Technical Education Council) Leisure Studies course. This is a general foundation in Leisure, and may include modules on Arts and Entertainment, Sport and Physical Recreation, Hospitality, Tourism, Cultural Recreation and Countryside.

/ ACTIVITY /

All jobs include less attractive elements, as you can see. In order that you may get to know yourself better, ask yourself the following:

1 Which duties do you find attractive or easy to accomplish in the above job description?

2 Which duties would you find difficult to undertake?

3 Make a list for each question and give reasons for your answers.

The BTEC First Diploma is a one-year course, which leads onto the two-year National Diploma course. Alternative entry requirements for the National are four GCSE's grade C or above. The National Diploma in Leisure Studies also entitles you to proceed to Higher Education and can therefore be considered as an alternative course to A-levels.

What can Higher Education offer me?

There are many courses in Leisure Studies or related objects such as Tourism, Catering, Amenity Horticulture, Hotel Management and Water-based Leisure, etc. Higher National Diplomas tend to be more vocational than degrees, which may make it slightly easier to gain entry to leisure posts.

How do I become a Manager?

Relevant qualifications will help to get you on to a trainee scheme, but these are not always easily available, as there are far more basic jobs available than management. Experience is still valued very highly, and 'working your way up' is a common route to management. Large national and multinational companies such as Mecca, Rank, Butlins, Trusthouse Forte and Olympus Sports, are worth investigating.

Professional qualifications in Leisure Management

The Institute of Leisure and Amenity Management offers relevant Certificate and Diploma courses for managers which are accessible by various learning methods.

Further information

Careers information is available from:

The Sports Council
16 Upper Woburn Place
London WCIH 0QP
Tel 071 388 1277

Institute of Leisure and Amenity Management
ILAM House
Lower Basildon
Reading, Berkshire
Tel 0491 873558

The Handbook of Tourism and Leisure
(CRAC) Publication available in the reference/careers sections of most libraries.

Focus on the Amenities and Recreation Department, Houghton City Council

Figure 11.4 highlights a typical career path inside a local government department. However, promotion in local authorities is not always confined to the same department or the same local authority, and staff are expected to have a broad knowledge of the government structure as well as a range of skills that they can adapt and enhance to perform a certain job. In most places in-service training is supported by departments (for instance at a local further education college) subject to the local authority budget.

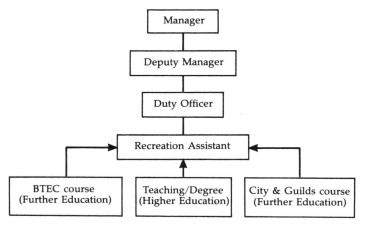

▲ *Figure 11.4   Houghton City Council: this extract from an organisation chart illustrates the post of Recreation Assistant and the qualifications required for the job*

We interviewed a local government employee, Julie Ferguson, in the Amenities and Recreation Department, regarding her career and got the following response:

I joined the Local Government service when I left school in the early 1970s at the age of 16. I was impressed with the structure for progression and the salary scales at the time for school leavers with five GCSEs. There were 20 of us on an integrated training programme at County Hall and we were expected to work in at least four different departments during the first six months' probation period, before settling into a career in one of them.

During the period of the two years' training, I was given day release to complete a Public Administration course at the local technical college, which I was told was the equivalent of two GCE A-levels. I was quite lucky, because after six months I settled in the Clerks Department (really the department for general administration of the whole of the Council) and eventually gained the National Certificate at college (now known as the BTEC National Certificate in Public Administration).

When the City Council at City Hall created an Amenities Department I was interested and was able to transfer to a job as a Clerical Officer in the Recreation Department (a sub-department of the Amenities Department). It was on a slightly higher scale and involved assisting the Recreation Development Officer in starting to categorise all types of recreation around the city. Eventually the whole department expanded to include tourism and entertainment.

I am now an Assistant City Amenities and Recreation Officer in charge of Parks and Recreation, a position on a senior level. Many of my colleagues have left the service for jobs in leisure in the private sector. The main reason was that they felt these jobs gave them more scope to put their ideas into practice. To my mind local government has changed so much in recent years that there is plenty of scope here, for instance, compulsory competitive tendering and so on, so I hope to continue my career in local government.

I believe that it is harder for young people to obtain a 'foot on the ladder' in local government and in many authorities training programmes have been cut back, but it is still possible to obtain a career even though one might have to study full time at college after school and go into the work environment at 18 rather than straight from school as I did. In fact there are far more relevant qualifications on offer now, such as the BTEC National or First Course in Leisure Studies.

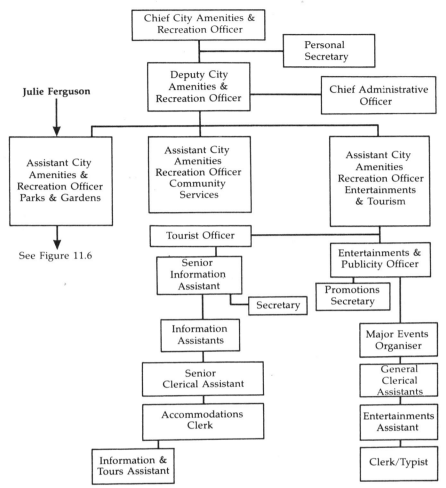

▲ *Figure 11.5   Houghton City Council: city amenities organisation chart showing the three main subsections: Parks & Gardens, Community Services and Entertainments & Tourism*

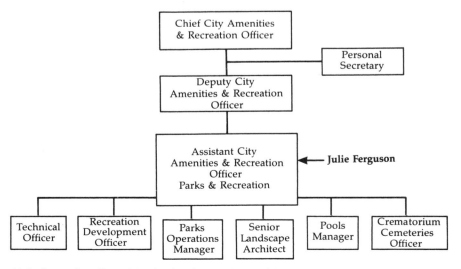

▲ *Figure 11.6   Extract from Figure 11.5 showing the organisation of the city amenities Parks & Gardens section*

Arrange to interview an employee in the leisure environment and write a profile of their career path to date.

Summary

▶ Managers in leisure-based organisations must be capable of organising their work, solving problems, planning ahead, delegating tasks, and supporting their staff.

▶ Organisations are often run on a teamwork basis, led by a manager. Each member of the team is an important part of the organisation and must offer his or her specific skills to co-operate with others.

▶ Motivation and positive attitudes are necessary to enable the organisation as a whole to achieve its aims and provide a service to its customers.

▶ The career paths in leisure are varied, interesting and increasingly more numerous because leisure itself is far more important today. There are many more educational courses on offer which are relevant to those students who wish to obtain not just work, but a career in leisure.

▶ The leisure environment can be a fun, innovative, and rewarding sector to work in because it deals with people's enjoyment and relaxation.

Assignment 8

JOB SURVEY

Conduct a survey of jobs in the leisure industry over the period of a week. You should include local and national newspapers and specialist publications, such as *Leisure Opportunities* (advertising public sector posts).

1 Classify the jobs into public, private or voluntary sector.

2 List the most commonly required qualities/qualifications.

3 What information can you ascertain about working conditions and salaries?

4 Choose a job in which you are interested and write a letter of application and a curriculum vitae. You should then conduct a 'mock interview' with another member of the group, which should be videoed if possible. During the interview, you will need to be able to talk about what skills you have to offer, why you have applied for the job, what you know about the organisation, etc. You should also be prepared to ask questions about training possibilities, or working conditions.

Assignment 9

MANAGING PEOPLE PROBLEMS
Role play

You are the manager of a leisure centre and need to solve the following problems. Your partner should assume one of the staff roles (see Appendix 2, page 169). You may take it in turns to be the manager. When you have done this you are required to appraise how you handled the situation (alternatively the appraisal may be carried out by an observer) and describe the management style you used (a management assessment form is shown overleaf to assist you). What difficulties do you face when trying to solve the problem and how might you react when faced with a similar problem in the future?

Management assessment

Name _____

	1	2	3	4	5
Listening skills					
Non-verbal communication (NVC)					
Appropriate use of language					
Manner					
Ability to ask relevant questions					
Problem solving					
Decision making					

General comments

Notes
The observer should tick the relevant box.
1 = Low   5 = High

▲ *Figure 11.7   Management assessment form*

National and international influences on leisure

Aims

▶ To trace national and international influences on leisure
▶ To look at current trends and possible future developments

The growth of leisure

Confidence that the leisure industry will continue to expand and develop into the 1990s continues. In Chapter 9 we explored the socio-economic trends in society which indicate the growing demand for leisure provision as people have more free time on their hands and more disposable income to spend on leisure pursuits. Technological advances have influenced the development of the leisure industry which in recent years has seen the proliferation of computerised fitness training equipment, animatronics, such as life-size robots, and spectacular attractions, e.g. Disneyland. The demands of consumers are becoming correspondingly sophisticated.

Theme parks

Theme parks continue to be a major growth area. By combining imagination and technology they appear to succeed in baffling, amusing, thrilling, enchanting and delighting their visitors. Disneyland in the USA was one of the original attractions of this kind and now the UK is well served by theme parks such as Alton Towers in Staffordshire, Thorpe Park in Surrey and Chessington World of Adventure, also in Surrey. Table 12.1, page 122 lists the most popular tourist attractions and illustrates the popularity of themed attractions.

The UK also has a lot to offer in the way of industrial, historical and maritime heritage, and these types of attractions are particularly attractive to overseas visitors.

ACTIVITY

1 Look at Table 12.1 on the following page and identify the 'heritage' attractions.

2 Select two or three of the attractions listed which may be known to you and list the reasons why that particular attraction is popular.

3 Select one attraction which you are not familiar with and find out about it. Collect samples of publicity. If possible, arrange a visit to sample the attraction at first hand!

Table 12.1   Attendances at the most popular tourist attractions

	1981	1986	1987	*Millions* 1988
Attractions with free admission				
Blackpool Pleasure Beach	7.5	6.5	6.5	6.5
British Museum	2.6	3.6	3.7	3.8
Albert Dock, Liverpool		2.0	3.1	3.5
National Gallery	2.7	3.2	3.6	3.2
Science Museum	3.8	3.0	3.2	2.4
Pleasure Beach, Gt Yarmouth				2.3
Tate Gallery	0.9	1.1	1.7	1.6
Pleasureland, Southport			1.1	1.5
Bradgate Park	1.2	1.2	1.2	1.2
Stapeley Water Gardens, Cheshire		1.0	1.0	1.0
Attractions charging admission				
Madame Tussaud's[1]	2.0	2.4	2.4	2.7
Alton Towers	1.6	2.2	2.3	2.5
Tower of London	2.1	2.0	2.3	2.2
Blackpool Tower		1.4	1.5	1.5
Natural History Museum[2]	3.7	2.7	1.6	1.4
London Zoo	1.1	1.2	1.3	1.3
Kew Gardens	0.9	1.1	1.3	1.2
Magnum Leisure Centre, Irvine		1.3	1.1	1.1
Thorpe Park	0.6	1.1	1.1	1.0
Flamingo Land, North Yorkshire		0.9	0.9	1.0

1 1988 figure not comparable with previous years
2 Admission charges were introduced in April 1987

From *Social Trends 20* 1990
© Crown Copyright 1990

Much of leisure development is taking place in the private sector, as large commercial organisations with hitherto no connections with leisure are diversifying into certain areas of the industry. The potential profits to be recouped from investing in large leisure complexes, such as Brighton Marina, are enormous.

It is important to remember that tourism is a leisure activity, and is therefore closely linked to the leisure industry. Many of the examples given in this chapter may be categorised as tourist attractions; it is impossible to disassociate the two when considering the leisure environment because day trips, visits to theme parks, museums, etc. are freely undertaken in people's leisure time!

▶
*Great Yarmouth
leisure complex, Norfolk*

National influences on leisure

Climate

National Tourist Boards have long recognised the necessity for more indoor leisure complexes, especially in seaside resorts. If Britain is to compete successfully with Mediterranean holiday destinations, visitors to UK holiday resorts must be provided with undercover recreation facilities so that tourists have an alternative to the beach when it rains. More and more resorts are responding to this need, especially as many of them are seeking to expand the tourist season into the autumn months. Large leisure centres with wet and dry sections, including leisure pools, are features of many seaside resorts, e.g. Great Yarmouth Marina Centre.

Centre Parcs was originally owned by a Dutch company, but was recently taken over by Scottish and Newcastle Brewers. Centre Parcs has taken the idea of year round leisure complexes one step further by providing visitors with a 'tropical paradise' environment where the temperature is a constant 84 °F, regardless of the weather outside! The most characteristic feature of this development is a large 60 metre wide, 220 metre high dome which houses the 'paradise' and even allows visitors to get a suntan. The complexes built in the UK so far have been a huge success and there are plans for further developments in the UK and northern Europe.

Government policy and influence – regeneration

As areas of the country where traditional industries, such as manufacturing and heavy industry, have declined the Government has encouraged economic regeneration through the development of the service sector. Examples of such developments are the Albert Docks in Liverpool, and Portsmouth Harbour dockland area. The decline of the Docklands in Portsmouth prompted the development of a Maritime Heritage Centre, featuring ships such as the *Mary Rose*, the *Victory*, the *Warrior* and a maritime museum.

In Brighton the Marina Complex, developed by the Brent Walker group, has been built on totally reclaimed land. A village has been created around the marina with a variety of shops, pubs, restaurants, flats and houses. Further developments include a hotel and leisure complex, sports centre, health hydro, water theme park, multi-screen cinema and nightclub. The development aims to cater for locals and for people visiting the Marina by boat.

The Albert Docks in Liverpool has also been successfully developed and is now a focal point for visitors to the city. There is a maritime museum with a unique display on emigration from the port. Much of the development utilises warehouses no longer needed as a result of the decline of Liverpool as a port. In addition, there is a range of specialist shops and restaurants.

Bradford, once a booming textile town, is now using its industrial heritage as a theme to attract visitors for short breaks by offering tours of the old mills, canal trips, and by exploiting the connexions with nearby Brontë country.

The Channel Tunnel
The Channel Tunnel, a scheme initiated by the British and French governments, due to be completed in 1992, will increase the number of visitors to attractions in the UK and will also enable British visitors to gain easier access to attractions in Europe, e.g. Euro Disney, near Paris.

Privatisation
The privatisation of water has resulted in control of reservoirs (where water-based leisure is important) being relinquished to the private sector. Users of these facilities are concerned that commercialisation may restrict their access and result in increased prices. Government watchdog committees aim to represent consumer interests.

▲ *The Albert Dock development, Liverpool*

Compulsory competitive tendering

The 1988 Local Government Bill has had an immense effect on the management and running of all local authority leisure facilities (as explained in Chapter 5).

Other national trends

Swimming pools

The 'leisurisation' of swimming pools has been taking place gradually over the last few years. Leisure pools concentrate on the 'fun' aspects of water, through the use of flumes, jacuzzis and internal landscaping with plants. The emphasis is on family fun; the actual time spent swimming may be minimal. Some leisure pools have dry areas where children can play. The time spent in leisure pools tends to be longer than in traditional swimming pools, as there are more attractions on offer.

In some areas leisure pools pose a threat to the existence of the traditional rectangular lane pools, where 'serious' swimming takes place. Coaching organisations and swimming clubs tend to favour the traditional designs, arguing that it is difficult to teach effectively in round pools. Fitness swimmers also find it difficult to train in round pools.

Museums

In the past, a visit to a museum may have been a dull, passive experience for a child. Today, however, there are fewer straightforward museums and more 'experiences', 'stories', etc. on offer, which can make the idea of visiting a museum a much more attractive prospect. For example, the Jorvik Centre in York, has been imaginatively developed as a model Viking village, including sounds, scenes and characters of the day. The visitor is taken (by means of a mini train) on a passage through time and for a few minutes is given the opportunity to sample life as it was then. The idea of replicating living experiences has been so successful that Oxford has developed a similar attraction; the Oxford Experience. Similarly, the Royalty and Empire Museum in Windsor has recreated spectacular scenes from Victorian times. Using advanced computer technology, called animatronics, visitors are also able to watch a realistic 'live' play with Queen Victoria as the star! The advantage of using life-sized animatronic models rather than real actors is that they never get tired and are able to carry out innumerable performances in a day.

Hotels

Increasingly, hotels are offering off-peak short break holidays with leisure packages which include use of facilities such as the gymnasium, swimming pool, weight training room, squash courts, etc. Other hotels may offer theme weekends, e.g. 'Whodunit?', where guests are able to recreate an Agatha Christie novel for the weekend!

Factory tourism

Nowadays, industrial organisations are increasingly opening their doors to visitors. The nature of organisations preparing to welcome visitors varies from the Granada TV studios, to Fords of Dagenham.

In the future, visitors can expect to be offered spectacular attractions, such as rides exploring the history of the car, with simulations of travelling along a production line, complemented by audio-visual shows. Again the emphasis is on giving the visitor the opportunity to have a 'live experience', which is fun and also informative.

Leisure retailing

Shopping, or simply window shopping, is a major leisure activity, and large undercover shopping centres, attractively designed and landscaped, are a feature of an increasing number of British town centres.

Sports shops sell their goods not only to sports enthusiasts, but to the majority of the population who identify strongly with the casual sporty lifestyle image. Some sports shops claim that 80 per cent of their sales are to non-sporty people. For example, brightly coloured surf shorts, once confined to surfers, are now acceptable summer wear in towns. Racing cycling shorts have been accepted as leisure wear, and have also been adopted by aerobics enthusiasts. As fitness becomes increasingly fashionable, the spin-offs for retailing are enormous.

Another important aspect of leisure retailing is the travel agency. As more people are demanding more quality holidays, which offer more than just a beach holiday package, there is scope for the special interest tour, which can be anything from trekking in Nepal to a painting holiday in Britain. Some travel agencies will also organise tailor-made tours for groups or individuals.

ACTIVITY

1 Visit your local shopping centre and select two or three major high street stores. Make a note of the lines of 'leisure' clothes that are being promoted. What colours and styles are particularly in evidence?

2 Visit a local travel agency and look for any brochures which offer special interest holidays (e.g. skiing, water sports). Analyse the types of packages offered, in terms of range of resorts and holidays, prices, equipment provided, social programme, and user groups the brochure is targeting. Summarise your findings.

3 Look at the classified adverts in any Sunday quality newspaper. List the special interest companies who are advertising, e.g. safaris. Make a note of the particular appeal of each one. Who are they trying to attract?

Stress and today's society

Stress is caused by many factors, including commuting, being stuck in traffic jams, pressures of work and the necessity to succeed, plus the motivation to increase one's standard of living through earning more money, perhaps through gaining promotion.

As a result of this there are spin-offs for the leisure industry, where antidotes to stress are being offered in the form of relaxation, meditation and massage classes, together with 'stress management' and assertiveness training courses.

International influences on leisure

USA

It is often felt that whatever developments take place in the USA sooner or later the UK will be influenced by them. It appears that the 'special' political relationship which Britain is said to enjoy with the USA extends to the leisure industry. For example, we have adopted skateboarding, windsurfing, theme parks, aerobics classes, indoor shopping centres and garden centres from across the Atlantic. The sphere of influence is extended through the media, especially the film industry, where 'blockbuster' films promote new lifestyles. Advertising, such as that for cola drinks, also plays a part in transmitting a desirable image for young people to emulate.

ACTIVITY

Discuss any recent blockbuster films you have seen, and identify the potential influence that they may have on lifestyles. What message do they convey, if any?

The Americanisation of leisure

Private health clubs, which are big business in the States, are also becoming popular in the UK. Sophisticated equipment and marketing methods are being taken on board by British healthclubs. One example is the Barbican Club in London, which caters for young executives working in the City.

Alton Towers, Britain's biggest theme park, is modelled on Disneyland and, since its inception, theme parks have mushroomed in the UK. In recent years Jane Fonda has revolutionised aerobics classes in this country. Many women who previously undertook little or no exercise eagerly attended Jane Fonda workouts in order to get into shape! Some concern was subsequently expressed about the safety and intensity of the exercises, and as a result 'low-impact' aerobics have been introduced, based on a less strenuous routine.

Generally there has been a greater emphasis on exercising safely and walking has become popular in the States. As an antidote to stress, 'flotation' therapy, pioneered in the States in the

▲ *Disneyworld in Florida USA; an example of a trend in leisure which the UK has adopted*

1950s as a relaxation therapy, is increasing in popularity in Britain. The process entails the person floating in a tank of salty water in the dark in complete silence for an hour. This produces a state of deep relaxation, equivalent to several hours' sleep. For busy executives this could be a very beneficial experience.

Canada

In 1970 a group of Canadian developers introduced the IMAX cinema system after identifying a demand for a sophisticated visual experience from the giant screen cinema. The film is projected onto a larger domed screen which extends to the edge of the audience's peripheral vision as well as overhead. The audience has to move their eyes and heads in order to see the entire picture. An all-round experience is completed by having seating steeply raked so that the horizon appears in a natural position for most viewers. In an age when passive entertainment is so popular, the IMAX cinema can be described as the ultimate passive leisure activity. To date most of the IMAX installations are in heritage centres, theme parks, cultural centres, etc. but they are likely to become much more widespread in the future. In Britain, the National Museum of Film, Photography and Television in Bradford includes an IMAX cinema as an attraction, shown below.

European Community

As a member country of the EC, the UK has to fulfil certain safety measures, such as ensuring that polluted beaches meet EC safety standards within a specified time limit. In 1992, there will be easier access for any European companies to expand into Britain, opening the way for Europeanisation, which is likely to have an impact on the leisure industry. In West Germany, for instance, 'Freizeitzentrum' (literally 'free-time centres'), the equivalent to our leisure pools, were established long before the UK. West Germany also has a greater number of

▲ *The sophisticated visual experience of the IMAX cinema*

thermal spa pools available to the public; these are still somewhat of a rarity in the UK. In Germany preventative health care is big business, and spa centres are considered as part of this care. It is not uncommon for workers to be granted several weeks leave so that they can go on a 'cure' to a health farm/spa centre, for rest and relaxation. In Britain health farms are still relatively exclusive institutions.

Timeshare

Timeshare apartments which can be bought for a specified time period for a few weeks each year, have become very popular over the last few years. Timeshare developments started in Spain, where the developers clamoured to entice British customers. There have been a number of problems with Timeshare contracts, with owners having to pay steep service charges, etc. but the scheme has extended into the UK to areas such as the Lake District and Scotland.

/ **ACTIVITY** /

How does the UK compare with other members of the EC?   Look at the table below and analyse the different percentages of expenditure on leisure between EC countries. What are the implications for 1992? (Note: The proportion of household expenditure spent on health care in the UK and Denmark appears comparatively low because both countries provide 'free' care at the time of use, whereas other countries reimburse patients, who have to pay directly for treatment.)

Household expenditure patterns: EC comparison, 1986

	Food, beverages, tobacco %	Clothing and footwear %	Rent, fuel and power %	Furniture, furnishings, household equipment %	Medical care and health expenses %	Transport and communication %	Recreation, entertainment, education, culture %	Misc. goods and services %	Total %
United Kingdom	18.9	7.2	20.3	6.8	1.3	16.3	9.7	19.5	100.0
Belgium[1]	21.3	8.1	18.3	10.4	10.6	12.2	6.5	14.1	100.0
Denmark	23.5	6.0	25.1	6.8	1.8	17.4	9.6	9.8	100.0
France	20.5	7.2	18.7	8.5	8.9	16.4	7.2	12.6	100.0
Germany (Fed. Rep)	17.0	8.1	19.0	8.4	14.2	14.5	8.9	9.8	100.0
Greece	39.9	8.6	11.6	8.2	2.9	15.0	4.5	9.3	100.0
Irish Republic[1]	43.2	6.4	12.4	6.5	2.6	13.0	9.1	6.9	100.0
Italy	24.5	9.1	14.9	8.6	5.5	12.6	8.4	16.3	100.0
Luxembourg[1]	23.3	6.6	21.0	9.2	6.7	16.9	3.4	12.9	100.0
Netherlands	19.1	7.3	19.4	7.5	12.7	10.9	9.5	13.6	100.0
Portugal[2]	37.9	9.2	5.3	8.9	4.4	15.5	5.6	13.1	100.0
Spain	27.2	7.2	15.2	7.1	3.4	13.9	6.7	19.2	100.0

1 Percentages add to more than 100 because of a statistical adjustment to total expenditure
2 1985

From *Social Trends 19* 1989
© Crown Copyright 1989

Eastern Block

Before the advent of 'Perestroika' the influence of Eastern Block countries was limited to a few world famous organisations such as the Moscow State Circus and the Bolshoi Ballet. Brilliant gymnasts and athletes produced by these countries so impressed the West that some attempt was made to emulate the schools of excellence for sport which produced these athletes. This had limited success due to lack of state funding – in the East, these schools of sport were totally state funded.

More recently, a greater number of exchanges between city orchestras, ballet companies and other organisations have been encouraged between former Eastern Block countries and the UK. The unification of East and West Germany works to the mutual exchange of leisure ideas.

International events

Major events such as the Olympics often popularise a sport if a national team or player is successful. For example, as a result of the British hockey team winning a gold medal, hockey now has more media coverage and an increased number of recruits for the sport.

Similarly, tennis players such as Steffi Graf and Boris Becker, both of whom have won Wimbledon titles, have encouraged more young people to take up tennis in their country.

In the arts world film festivals, such as Berlin and Cannes, where various awards are given, can have a major impact on the future success of any film. A bad review may jeopardise the subsequent popularity of the film when it goes 'on circuit'.

The Edinburgh Festival of music, theatre and dance is seen as a potential stepping stone to greater things for productions from all over the world. A number of productions begin there before transferring to London's West End.

In Montreux, Switzerland, the acclaimed annual international rock festival gives a range of old and new performers the opportunity to publicise themselves to an international audience.

ACTIVITY

1 Investigate one of the major national or international influences on leisure which have been mentioned in the text.

2 Research any statistics and secondary information available, and write a short report summarising your findings.

Summary

▶ The impact of national and international influences on the leisure industry is far reaching.
▶ Government policy, the Local Government Bill and privatisation policies have all influenced the future of leisure provision.
▶ Leisure in the UK has been influenced by developments in other countries. The Americanisation of leisure is a notable aspect of this.
▶ Major international events, such as the Olympics, are potential vehicles for encouraging better international relations, and for stimulating more interest in certain activities.
▶ Theme parks, indoor leisure complexes, leisure pools, and similar entertainment are an important part of the current leisure lifestyle in the West. As the Eastern Block countries remove the political barriers they may also follow this trend.

13 / *Marketing of leisure*

Aims

▶ To outline the role of marketing and its relevance to leisure.
▶ To identify key marketing mix elements.
▶ To explain the meaning of SWOT analysis.

What is marketing?

Marketing can be defined as 'the activities involved in getting the right product to the right people at the right time in the right place'. Another definition is 'Marketing is concerned with the satisfaction of customers' needs, at the same time as making a profit.' There are many other definitions of marketing, but as far as the leisure industry is concerned, satisfying customer needs is the most important part of the marketing philosophy, because satisfied customers will always come back.

Regardless of whether organisations are in the public, private or voluntary sector, it is vital that a marketing philosophy is adopted. This may be initiated from a marketing department if one exists, but even the smallest of leisure organisations can address themselves to finding out what customers want, and keeping abreast of changing customer needs.

Butlins Holiday Centres, originally known as holiday camps, provided cheap, basic family holidays in the 1930s and 1940s but this type of holiday was less attractive to the more sophisticated customer of the 1970s. Hence, in order to survive, the organisation responded by investing in refurbishment programmes, updating facilities and accommodation, as well as adopting a more flexible approach in the daily running of the centres.

In response to changing needs a well-known hotel chain perceived that there was a significant increase in the number of businesswomen using their hotels. As a result certain rooms were specifically marketed to these customers; the decor was changed and made more feminine and hair-dryers and other extras were supplied. By identifying the changes in the market the hotel chain was able to target specifically at these women, who may otherwise have gone to another hotel.

The marketing mix

The marketing mix refers to the ingredients of marketing – the activities which are controlled by the organisation – and can be identified as the practical tools of marketing.

The elements of the marketing mix which are particularly relevant to the leisure industry are:

● Product development
● Price
● Market segmentation and research
● Promotion
● Public relations
● Personal selling.

131

The way that the organisation operates these elements varies according to different situations:

1 An up-market health club may well attract the type of customers it wants by setting high prices; once the club is established, customer care will be the main focus of the marketing activities.
2 In the 1980s when British Airways was privatised, a 'Putting People First' philosophy was emphasised: every employee underwent customer-care training with emphasis on the importance of putting the customer first. This customer care philosophy contributed significantly to the currently profitable state of British Airways.
3 A touring theatre company will need to ensure that plenty of publicity leaflets and posters are on display prior to the tour, together with local advertising.

Let us now examine elements of the marketing mix more closely.

Product development

The leisure product consists of a set of satisfactions which are delivered to the customer. The satisfactions consist of atmosphere, quality of facilities, friendliness of staff, image, etc. Leisure is a service product as is tourism, banking, and insurance. Examples of leisure products include sports goods, membership of a health club, theatre or concert tickets, or a particular type of holiday.

Brand names

Some products have brand names, such as Nike or Raleigh, which give them a strong identity. Well known brand names are usually the result of heavy investment in advertising and promotion. It is advantageous to have a product with strong branding because customers will often feel confident in purchasing a product with which they feel familiar.

Quality

The quality of the product is particularly important in the leisure industry: fast food chains such as McDonalds pride themselves on offering the same standard, high-quality burgers, all over the world. A person purchasing a ticket to a rock concert (a leisure product) will expect quality of performance. However, the quality of the greeting by the ushers and ticket collectors, and the level of service from the refreshment stall at the interval both play an important function in the overall experience of the customer. If one element lacks quality the whole experience will be marred, and the level of customer satisfaction will be reduced. It is notable that people now in their 30s and 40s who regularly attended rock concerts when they were teenagers now expect better quality all round when they go to a concert. In their teens, a quick pint at the bar may have been sufficient refreshment, whereas a pre-concert meal for two may now be the normal standard expected.

Cheap package holidays, in plentiful supply in the 1980s, were of poor quality and resulted in many complaints to travel agencies and tour operators. In the 1990s the trend is towards fewer operators but better quality holidays.

Options

Some products offer different options, such as the stalls or the circle in a theatre, or different types of seat on an aeroplane. There may be optional membership schemes of a health club, with the choice of the cheaper off-peak membership, family membership, or full membership.

Offering options should lead to greater customer satisfaction. However, if too many options are offered it may be financially risky for the organisation.

Product development

Product development needs to be an ongoing process, because people's needs are constantly changing and products need to respond to this. In the bicycle market, for example, the mountain bike evolved (in addition to other products in the range, e.g. touring, racing, shopping) because a demand arose for a bicycle suitable for riding in mountains and on rough terrain. In the tourism market, recent trends indicate that people want more independence and flexibility when they book package holidays. As a result, tour operators have responded by developing the traditional package holidays and offering more self-catering accommodation, fly/drive deals, etc.

/**ACTIVITY**/

Choose a leisure product, e.g. type of holiday, sports equipment, membership of a club, theatre performance. Which of the following elements are important in relation to the product?

- Brand name
- Options
- Product development
- Quality

Give examples of how these elements relate to the product.

Price

Getting the price right is not always an easy task. Different sectors of the industry have different aims: the voluntary sector and public sector will not necessarily be aiming to make a profit, whereas the commercial sector has a definite profit motive, and these factors will be reflected in the pricing policy.

When deciding what price to charge, there are several factors which the organisation must bear in mind:

- What costs have to be met? This includes fixed costs such as heating, lighting, transportation and staff salaries, and may include variable costs, such as raw materials (e.g. the metal used for manufacturing the bicycle).
- Government legislation, such as VAT (Value Added Tax). Organisations which are registered charities pay a reduced sum, under government legislation for business rates so this cost saving may be passed on to consumers, e.g. The National Trust.
- Peak or off-peak. In times when there is a higher demand, such as the summer season in the holiday market, or evenings and weekends in the health club market, higher prices are usually charged.
- What is the customer willing to pay? This may depend on the image, so that an up-market image will command higher prices. Or, if the product is a rare commodity, such as a performance by the Bolshoi Ballet in this country, people may be willing to pay higher prices for the privilege of a ticket.
- The number of people forecast to buy the product. For example, if it is perceived that a concert will be a sell-out, then pricing can be based on the maximum number of seats in the venue. If, however, it is envisaged that only half the seats will be sold, then the cost of tickets may be higher.
- Risk factor. New products often carry a high risk of failure, due to lack of initial market research. As many new products involve a lot of initial investment, high prices may be set initially in order to recoup it.

Pricing policies

1 **Market skimming** This policy can be used for products which are new, and do not have any real competition. A high price is charged which should attract people who do not mind paying higher prices for the privilege of being first to try the product. They are known as innovators. Once the product has been adopted by them the market has been 'skimmed',

and the price will gradually be reduced until it is at an affordable price for a wider range of consumers. Compact disc players, video recorders and home computers are all examples of products which have used the market skimming policy.

2 **The going rate**   Where there is a high degree of similarity between one organisation's product and another, the pricing policy may be based on the 'going rate'. An example of this would be two cinemas in one town, where ticket prices are similar. In the holiday market, competitive pricing of this kind is often used by tour operators who promise to match their prices to any other operators if a customer finds a similar competitive holiday which is cheaper.

3 **Penetration pricing**   When launching a new product in a highly competitive market, artificially low prices may be set initially, to entice the public to try the product. The aim is to win a large market share and earn more revenue from high sales. It is also hoped that the customers will remain brand loyal, even if the price later increases. However, it is possible that they will return to their former brand, or that they will be enticed by other new products.

Penetration pricing is often used for products known as 'fast moving consumer goods' (FMCGs), e.g. food, where consumers are particularly sensitive to prices. In recent years, penetration pricing has also been successfully used by large tour operators, with the result that price wars have put some companies out of business.

4 **Promotional pricing**   Examples of this policy include offering 'two for the price of one'; money-off coupons; reductions for bulk buying, e.g. tickets for a series of concerts, instead of one; a free item, e.g. a free towel with membership to a health club.

5 **Reduced prices**   Prices may be marked down if a product fails to sell sufficiently. In London, for example, it is possible to buy half-price theatre tickets on the day of the performance. It is obviously better for a theatre to fill seats, albeit at reduced prices, in order to increase the revenue. Tour operators also use this strategy by marking down the cost of unsold holidays a few days before they are due to commence. These are offered under various names, i.e. 'Square Deals'. In the 1980s these bargains were fairly common, but as the total number of holidays on offer has been reduced there is less likely to be excess supply in the 1990s.

6 **Prestige pricing**   Where products have a high quality or exclusive appeal, high prices can be set, based on the assumption that people associate high prices with high quality. Hence, health clubs with exclusive images can command high prices. Similarly, people booking holidays which have a suggestion of luxury will expect to pay high prices, because that is part of the appeal! If the holidays were sold cheaply, they would lose their exclusive image and therefore become less attractive.

Prestige pricing is often used for perfumes and aftershaves, where an exclusive image is very important.

7 **Payment**   Nowadays, there is an emphasis on making it as easy as possible for the customer to pay for the product. Hence, credit card booking for theatre tickets is normal practice. Payment by installments for membership schemes is often an alternative to a one-off lump payment. Often customers are encouraged to pay by direct debit from their bank accounts, where a sum of money is deducted monthly from their account, automatically. This is advantageous for the organisation, as there is a greater guarantee that the payment is made, rather than relying on the customer to write a cheque and send it every month.

ACTIVITY

Which pricing policies would you use for the following products? Why?

- A week at an exclusive health farm
- A new cheap quality training shoe
- A portable TV
- Tickets for an amateur dramatic production at the community centre

Market segmentation

In Chapter 9 we looked at different user groups. In marketing terms, dividing the market up into different segments is important because leisure organisations need to target their products and services to specific target groups. Ways of segmenting the market include categorisation by socio-economic groups, housing types, age, sex, lifestyle, etc. (see Chapter 9).

Psychographic segmentation is a more abstract method of categorising the market. Rather than being based on facts and figures, it is more concerned with people's personality and behaviour type.

Advertisers sometimes rely on the 'five Cs' method of segmentation. This refers to five classes of people categorised by their needs and prime motivations.

The largest groups are:

1 **Mainstreamers** comprise about 40 per cent of the population. They are motivated to belong and to feel secure. Hence, they are very attracted to branded products.

2 **Aspirers**, on the other hand, are motivated by status and money. They do not worry about security, but are attracted to status symbols such as expensive cars, hi-fis and Rolex watches! They frequently use credit cards, read the latest magazines and participate in the latest sports.

3 **Succeeders** like being in control. They have achieved their ambitions and are often in positions of power. They may be slightly autocratic.

4 **Reformers** tend to be those who buy own brand rather than branded products. They are the most educated group, often motivated by self-fulfillment, and they wish to influence society, and are therefore more likely to be on committees and to join conservation/ environmental groups.

5 **Individuals** like to feel independent and have their own individual style.

Some psychographic terminology has been absorbed into everyday vocabulary: Yuppies (Young Upwardly-Mobile Professionals), Yappies (Young Affluent Parents), Dinkies (Double Income, No Kids), Woopies (Working Older People), Sloane Rangers, IDBs (In Daddy's Business), are examples you may be familiar with.

ACTIVITY

1 In pairs, discuss the meaning of the psychographic categories mentioned in the text, starting with Yuppie.

2 Construct a brief profile of the lifestyles for each group. Compare your results with others in the group.

Market research

In order to find out what customer needs are, there needs to be a process of ongoing **feedback** from the consumer.

How do you get feedback? Before launching a product, there needs to be some form of market research carried out. For example, a leisure centre proposes to add a sauna to its facilities. First, it is a good idea to look at any data about saunas that has already been published. This may be in the form of statistics relating to usage, reports, articles in magazines, etc. This type of information is known as **secondary data** and can often be purchased from market research organisations.

Once this background data is obtained, you may wish to carry out a **sample survey**. This may involve devising a questionnaire and distributing it to a sample of existing or potential customers. The feedback from this type of original research is known as **primary data**. There are various types of samples which can be selected, but market researchers most often choose a **quota** sample. This means that a number of people are pre-selected to be included in the sample, so that it is representative as far as possible.

For example, the health club proposing to add a sauna to its facilities, would possibly include in the sample a quota of:

● Single males
● Single females
● Married males
● Married females.

The quota could be further subdivided into age groups, socio-economic groups, etc. For example:

● Single males, aged 18–34
● Single males, aged 34–50
● Single males, aged 50+.

The number of respondents to be included in each quota depends on how well represented they are in the health club membership. For example, if single males aged 18–34 are the biggest group, comprising 30 per cent of the members, then this should be reflected in their quota size. Therefore, if the total sample is 100, the quota of males aged 18–34 to be included is 30. The advantage of using a quota sample is that it combines reasonable accuracy with cost effectiveness.

Carrying out the survey

Consideration needs to be given as to the most efficient way of reaching the respondents in the sample. In the case of the health club survey about the feasibility of adding a sauna, the following methods may be used:

1 **Personal interviews**   Although interviews are time consuming and are the most costly method because they are labour-intensive, it is possible to go into more depth. Care must be taken that the interviewer does not introduce any bias. He or she should be as objective as possible when interviewing, and show no reaction to any of the responses.

2 **Mail surveys**   The advantage here is that all parts of the country can be reached at the same time for the cost of a stamp. However, there are disadvantages, such as the **response** rate, which tends to be lower. The response rate may be improved if stamped addressed envelopes are supplied, and it may be necessary to send several reminder letters.

3 **Telephone surveys**   These are useful for gathering feedback very quickly from topical events: calls generally last between 5 and 10 minutes.

Other forms of feedback

- Customer complaints box
- Internal statistics, such as sales turnover for each product
- Computerised entry systems, which give breakdowns regarding the numbers, ages, etc. of each user at any particular time
- Contacting customers who have not used the facility for a while to find out why. NB: This may be more feasible in a private venture
- Trained staff who are encouraged to listen and take note of customer suggestions. These suggestions should then be communicated at team meetings.

/ACTIVITY/

1 Select a leisure facility and arrange an interview with the manager.

2 Find out what he or she knows about the organisation's customers, and what type of marketing research activities are carried out. What are your conclusions?

Promotion

One of the most successful ways of promoting a product is through word of mouth. Satisfied customers will recommend your product to others and this is far more influential than money spent on advertising, etc. However, most organisations do not only rely on word of mouth, but actively seek to promote their products and services.

Promotional activities include:

- Advertising
- Public relations
- Sales promotions
- Personal selling.

Advertising

What are the functions of advertising?

- To create awareness, e.g. for new products
- To give information, e.g. on modifications to existing products such as theatre tickets, which include an evening meal prior to the performance.
- To create a 'Unique Selling Proposition'. The aim of this strategy is to differentiate your product/service from competitors, i.e. to identify a unique characteristic of the product or service, e.g. a confectionery such as Polo uses a USP strategy by advertising the fact that it is the only mint sweet with a hole in the middle! In leisure terms an example of a USP would be emphasising a particularly attractive location or feature, such as the Domed Tropical Paradise in Centre Parcs holiday complexes (see Chapter 12).
- To remind, e.g. after initial advertising people need to be regularly reminded that your product exists, or competitive products may 'interfere'.

Media selection

How do you decide which media to use? There are advantages and disadvantages with every media choice. Table 13.1 illustrates some of the more general points:

Table 13.1 Media selection

Advantages	Disadvantages
Television	
Dynamic	Expensive
Mass markets	
Posters	
Back-up to TV campaign	Not always easy to measure their success
Create awareness	
Newspapers	
Targeting to specific markets	Static readership numbers
National or local papers	
Cinema	
Useful for younger markets	Repetition may be a problem (infrequent attendance
Relatively cheap	by audience)
Commercial radio	
Good for local markets	Possibly restricted age groups of listeners
Cheap	

/ **ACTIVITY** /

Choose one of the methods of promotion mentioned and, over a period of one week, monitor the type of products which the medium is advertising. How many of these are leisure products?

Public relations

Organisations obviously wish to communicate a positive image; e.g. a 'caring for the community' image, which creates goodwill locally, and positively benefits the organisation. An example of a public relations activity would be a charity football match to raise money for a new piece of equipment for the local hospital. Sponsorship of local events, such as festivals or half marathons, is also a public relations activity.

Public relations activities are concerned with the image the organisation wishes to convey both internally (to employees), and externally to the general public.

Who is the 'public'?
The public, as far as any organisation is concerned, includes:

- Employees
- The local community
- Shareholders
- Current and future customers
- Suppliers
- The media, e.g. newspapers.

We shall briefly examine some of the public relations channels which are used to communicate with the 'public'.

Public relations channels
Internal
- Noticeboards
- Staff magazine/newsletter
- Annual Report

External
- Noticeboards
- Press conferences – used to brief the press on new developments within the company
- Press releases – information sent to the press with the aim of getting free publicity

- Feature articles in newspapers/magazines – detailed news items, often illustrated with pictures and/or diagrams
- Company videos – documentaries about the company
- Sponsorship of events – company sponsors events in return for free publicity
- Exhibitions, e.g. world travel market, where organisations have a stand with a display publicising their products.

/ACTIVITY/

1 Make a note of which sector of the public an organisation is communicating with when using each of the public relations channels listed above (e.g. noticeboards: employees, customers, suppliers).

2 Look through back copies of the local newspaper and find examples of feature articles, and any other news features which exemplify public relations activities by a local leisure organisation. Summarise your findings and give feedback to the rest of your group.

3 Arrange a visit to any local leisure facility and interview the manager to find out what public relations activities the organisation has been involved with. How successful were they?

Social marketing

This is concerned with issues which are currently seen as important by society. Examples of social issues include: protection of the environment and green issues; animal rights and leading healthier lifestyles, illustrated by Health Education campaigns (see page 140, the leaflet: *Look After Yourself*), and Sports Council campaigns (*Sport for All*). As consumers become increasingly concerned with the state of the environment the responsibility of 'social marketing' is being taken on board by commercial enterprises in their promotion campaigns. The demand for products which are not detrimental to the environment is increasing rapidly. Tescos supermarket have a strong 'Healthy Eating' campaign, exemplified by their emphasis on high fibre and low fat products. The signs are that the consumer society of the 1980s is giving way to a much more caring, environmentally concerned society in the 1990s. Companies who do not respond to current social issues may do so at their peril!

Sales promotions

A new leisure centre has opened in the town and the manager advertises its presence by distributing various catalogues, leaflets and brochures, but in order to promote the various services offered, incentives are offered to members of the public to go along and join. For example:

- Discount schemes or price cuts for membership before a certain date.
- Demonstrations of the gym equipment on certain days, and free 'try out work out' sessions.
- Displays and exhibitions erected outside on opening day to show people the facilities.
- Advertisement in the local newspaper which includes a coupon offering a 10 per cent reduction for the sauna and solarium if used before a certain date.
- A local brewery offers to provide a challenge cup for a range of indoor sports, which is a form of sponsorship for the centre.
- Competitions held in the centre – for example 'Guess the Weight' in the multi gym and a 'Name that Sport' questionnaire; prizes may include a year's free membership and vouchers to be spent in the leisure and sports shop in the centre.
- All new members of staff are given an incentive to recruit members; for each new member they sign up they get a £10.00 bonus at the end of the month.

This type of sales promotion is known as 'below the line' or non-media advertising. In essence it induces people to try out or buy a particular service in the hope that they will continue to purchase it. It is often taken on by sales promotion companies, which specialise in launching new products and services and making existing ones more attractive to the public.

Sales promotions are regulated by law (see Chapter 5). These regulate how goods and services are promoted and how far a business can go in offering an inducement to buy their services.

Personal selling

In a people-centred industry, basic selling skills are essential. From a marketing point of view, personal selling philosophy is about 'helping people to buy', and not about selling people something they don't want.

Personal selling can be face to face or by telephone. There are many books which give detailed selling techniques; here we are concerned with basic planning of personal sales transactions. The key point about conducting successful sales interviews is in the planning process. Thorough planning will increase personal confidence, and prepare you (the seller) for any difficult questions which may arise.

How do you help people to buy?

Planning a sales interview

It is useful to plan any sales interview using a well-known selling model – AIDA (Attention, Interest, Desire and Action).

Attention   It is important to engage the customer's attention at the beginning. Avoid asking 'Can I help you?' This is a closed question, with a 50 per cent chance of a 'No' answer. It is better to say 'How can I help you?' Alternatively, interest may be created by offering 'Hello Mr Brown, I've got something to tell you about which I think will really interest you . . .'

Interest   It is necessary to find out about what the customer needs by asking open questions such as: 'What type of holiday are you looking for?' or 'How much exercise do you do?' These can be followed up by closed questions to obtain more specific answers: 'Do you want a hotel near the beach?' or 'Do you like to sit near the front, or nearer the back?' This method of questioning will help determine the person's needs. It is most important that you listen carefully to the answers. Make notes if necessary.

You can now begin to use your product knowledge to sell the benefits and features of the product, tailored to the particular customer. Benefits are statements which say what the product will do for the customer. Features are facts about the product. For example, a feature of a video recorder is that it can be programmed for 14 days ahead. A benefit is that you don't have to miss your favourite programmes when you are away on holiday.

A good salesperson will match relevant features to benefits, e.g. 'Our new leisure pool has a large flume slide, which means that the kids will have fun for hours'. The feature is the slide, but the benefit is the fun that it gives. It is important to connect the feature to the benefit, by using a useful phrase such as 'which means that'.

Very often an objection will be made, such as 'It is too expensive'. This indicates that you may not have emphasised enough benefits, so that the customer feels he or she is not getting value for money. It may be that the product would be more affordable if an easier method of payment (such as instalments) were offered. If a customer is really adamant about price objections, a cheaper alternative product could be offered: e.g. 'The seats in the stalls are cheaper' or 'We do have off-peak membership, which is half price'.

Desire   At this stage the customer should be giving **buying signals**. These may take the form of nodding the head approvingly, or making a statement which indicates that there is a desire for the product, e.g. 'Yes, I really think the facilities are marvellous', 'Well those seats look like they're in a reasonable position'. It is important that you learn to recognise buying signals, or the potential client may well leave and say 'I'll think about it'. Your aim is to secure some kind of commitment from the customer.

Action   There are many ways of closing sales: success may not mean a sale at this stage but an indication of commitment such as paying a deposit, or leaving a name and address.

ACTIVITY

A new leisure club has been set up and wishes to recruit corporate membership from local companies. You have made an appointment with the general manager of a new computer company, to tell him or her about your proposal.

Facts about the computer company
- 500 employees, mostly younger males
- Computer operators and programmers
- No on-site leisure facilities
- Social club exists but very basic, e.g. football and cricket team
- Manager is a keen sportsperson, who recently completed a half-marathon

Facts about the leisure club
- It has a team of qualified staff
- It is open from 7.30 a.m.–11 p.m. every day

- Facilities include weight room with up-to-date equipment, aerobics/dance studio, crèche facilities, sauna, steam room, jacuzzi, swimming pool, cafe/bar
- It is conveniently located in the industrial estate.

1 You are required to prepare the sales presentation, following the AIDA plan. Prepare your interview, using the following headings as guidelines:
   - 'Attention getting' opening sentence
   - Open and closed questions to establish needs
   - List of features and benefits
   - Possible objections, with answers
   - Action you wish the manager to take, e.g. complete a corporate membership form, visit the facility.

2 Record the conversation that might take place, which demonstrates the selling skills you have learned.

SWOT analysis

When a company reviews its position in the market, it often carries out a SWOT analysis prior to formulating a marketing plan. SWOT stands for:

- Strengths
- Weaknesses
- Opportunities
- Threats

For example, a **strength** may be that the company has a well-established name or that it is in a good location. A **weakness** could be that there is a low public awareness of the company's products. **Opportunities** may arise in expanding or exporting, or developing products. **Threats** could be in the form of competitors offering similar products, or external factors such as a depressed economy.

ACTIVITY

1 Focus on any local leisure organisation and carry out a SWOT analysis.

2 Choose a national leisure organisation, e.g. holiday company, hotel chain, or general leisure such as Mecca or Rank. Carry out a SWOT analysis using information obtained from reference books, the Annual Report and articles from magazines and newspapers.

Summary

▶ It is necessary to segment markets, and to carry out market research to keep abreast of people's changing needs.
▶ Important elements of the marketing mix outlined include price strategies, product elements, promotional aspects and personal selling.
▶ An introduction to social marketing should alert the reader to the important social issues which customers and organisations are concerned with.

Assignment 10

PLANNING AN EVENT

1 Organise an initial meeting, with the following agenda items:
   a) Allocation of roles and responsibilities (More than one person may be allocated to each role if necessary):
      - Co-ordinator
      - Administrator
      - Finance Officer
      - Marketing and Public Relations Officer
      - Safety Officer
      - Catering Officer.
   b) Nature of the event, e.g. fun run, disco, fête, jumble sale.
   c) Aims, if any, e.g. to raise money for charity?
   d) Details:
      - When
      - Where
      - Who for (user groups)
      - Numbers involved
      - Resources
      - Budgeting
      - Potential problems.

2 Plan out a weekly meeting schedule, where progress reports can be given and any problems discussed.

3 Draw up a general checklist of tasks within your responsibility, with a deadline date for completion of each task.
   Submit one copy of this to the co-ordinator.

4 Submit an informal report, outlining your role, with an evaluation of the outcome. Include all meeting minutes in the appendices, as well as copies of any letters, publicity, etc.

Assignment 11

THE VISITOR SURVEY

This assignment should be completed in conjunction with the owners of a local historic house or monument which is open for visitors, at least for the summer season. This will give you a clearer idea of how these places are run and how important they are in the leisure industry.

The aim of the survey is to find out detailed information regarding the visitors of the place; where they come from, why they visit, when they visit, how much they will pay for entrance fees and so on. You will need to gain the permission and assistance from the owners of the site, who may well be pleased to cooperate with you as they may be just as interested in the results of your survey.

It is suggested that the following details are arranged with the owners:

1 The dates of the survey (a two-week period should be sufficient in the summer months).
2 The actual days of the week the survey is to take place (weekends generate more visitors than weekdays, for obvious reasons).

3 The time of day the survey should take place.
4 The actual numbers of researchers and supervisors required.
5 The specific aims and objectives of the survey – for example, you must find out whether the survey is to improve the marketing image of the venue.
6 What kind of questions are to be asked (those that provoke short answers are best as they are less time consuming). A suggested questionnaire is provided below.
7 How the results of the survey are to be collated (charts, graphs, diagrams) and divided (male/female answers, age groups, occupations, percentages, averages, etc.). It might be useful to use a computer for the graphical diagrams.
8 How the results are best used – e.g. will they become public or are they for private use only?

Once the survey has been completed a report can be prepared on the results.

Suggested questionnaire: visitor survey

Good morning/afternoon. I am a Leisure Studies student at Cambridge Regional College and am carrying out a visitor survey on behalf of the National Trust. Would you mind answering a few questions, please?

1 Are you a member of the National Trust?   Yes ☐ No ☐

2 How many people are there in your party?   Over 18 ☐ Under 18 ☐

3 Is this your first visit to Wimpole?   Yes ☐ No ☐

   If yes go to question 5

4 How often have you been here before?   Once ☐ More than once ☐

5 Do you live in Britain?
   If yes: which county do you normally reside in? _____

   If no: which country do you normally reside in? _____

6 How far did you travel *today* to get to Wimpole?   Less than 10 miles
                                                               11–30 miles
                                                               More than 30 miles

7 How did you travel here?   Private car
                                                               Hired car
                                                               Group coach
                                                               Public transport
                                                               Other

8 How did you hear about Wimpole Hall?   National Trust literature
                                                      Tourist Information Centre
                                                      Newspaper advertising
                                                      Recommended by a friend
                                                      Other (please state) _____

9 Have you seen this leaflet before? (Show 'Nine Days Out' leaflet)

                                  Yes ☐ No ☐ Don't know ☐

10 Why did you decide to visit Wimpole today?   To see hall only
                                                      To see home farm only
                                              To see both hall and home farm
                                                           To see the park
                                                          To see everything

11 Overall, do you feel that the price you have paid to visit the property is:

Excellent value for money   Good value   No strong feelings   Poor value

Very poor value

12 Currently the National Trust does not charge visitors who only wish to see the grounds and the stables. Do you think that visitors who only wish to use these facilities would be prepared to pay a moderate car park charge?   Yes ☐ No ☐

13 Do you think that visitors wishing to see both the Hall and/or the Farm would be prepared to pay a moderate car park charge?   Yes ☐ No ☐

14 If an access charge were introduced, how much do you feel it would be reasonable to ask visitors to pay per vehicle?

50p
£1
More than £1

15 How would you describe your impressions of your visit to Wimpole?

Very enjoyable   Enjoyable   Indifferent   Unenjoyable   Very unenjoyable

16 Would you like to make any suggestions for improvements at this property?   Yes ☐ No ☐

If No, go to question 19

17 Could you briefly tell me what your suggestions are? _____

_____

18 What is your occupation? _____

19 Which age group do you fall into?

Under 18
18–34
35–44
45–54
55–64
65 and over

Thank you very much indeed for your help. Goodbye.

Is your interviewee   Male ☐   Female ☐

Assignment 12

THE NEW LEISURE DEVELOPMENT COMPANY

This broad-based assignment is designed to give practical assistance to students of leisure.

In order to complete the assignment you will need to research information specifically on the leisure industry, e.g. from sports and leisure magazines, sports equipment lists and Sports Council publications.

After completion of the assignment you might even want to try the whole process for real. However, remember that with any business one of the most important aspects is capital. Every year a large percentage of new businesses fail because they are under-capitalised and have cash flow problems (refer to the Department of Trade figures in your local library).

You have been working as a recreation officer at a leisure centre in a local town and have been head-hunted by a local business consortium which is keen to invest in the leisure industry. The management's knowledge of leisure is limited but they have recognised the growth potential in the market. They are looking to you for advice on the nature of the development. The sum to be invested is £1.5 million. The organisation is a private limited company.

You have been contracted for an initial period of six months to do the necessary groundwork.

1 Research and locate a suitable site and type of building in your area, stating the square footage and your justification for site selection.

2 Produce a plan of the development, incorporating the interior layout, with additional illustrations to show design, proposed colour scheme, lighting and methods of equipment to be used.

3 Investigate possible grant funding from appropriate bodies, e.g. Sports Council, Arts Council.

4 Draw up a cash flow, projected profit and loss and balance sheet for the first three years.

5 Give a cost breakdown of all the specialist equipment you need.

6 Draw up an initial organisation chart for the company. Detail your staffing requirements. Prepare a recruitment policy. Produce two sample job descriptions for key staff, with 'ideal candidates' profiles. Describe the management procedures which would be instituted, including your policy for management meetings, coffee breaks, holidays. Prepare a staff grievance procedure. Draw up a typical agenda for a senior management meeting which will take place six months from the opening date.

7 Produce a marketing plan for the first six months to include:
   a) Profile of the target market;
   b) Analysis of your competitors;
   c) Proposed pricing policy and membership scheme;
   d) Advertising and public relations activities, to include brochure of activities/ products offered;
   e) Indication of your ongoing market research activities;
   f) A brief on the facilities and restaurant/catering service to include menus;
   g) Budget breakdown of your marketing activities.

You are required to formulate your ideas into a formal report using the following headings:

- Concept
- Marketing
- Design
- Manpower
- Finance

You should also prepare an illustrative display board for an exhibition of the plans and be prepared to make a formal oral presentation of your findings.

RAINBOW UNITED FOOTBALL CLUB

Rainbow United Football Club is a private limited company, situated on the outskirts of a town (population 150 000). The principal activity of Rainbow United is that of a professional football club. It currently languishes in Division Four of the Football League. Spectrum Limited is a wholly-owned subsidiary company of Rainbow United; its main activity is the promotion of commercial ventures on behalf of the football club. Spectrum sells souvenirs, T-shirts, scarves, hats and associated items on the club's premises.

The club is struggling to survive financially; it has not had a great success rate in the League or Cup competitions; gate receipts have declined and it has been difficult to find sponsors. Last year no dividends were paid to shareholders. Furthermore the restructuring of the League has not helped clubs in the lower divisions. The company owns two minibuses which are used for the transportation of players to and from matches.

To alleviate financial difficulties a loan was secured from the local Town Council. However at a recent Board Meeting the directors decided that in order to secure long-term profitability a firm of management consultants should be called in. The management consultants' task is to appraise the current situation.

Assume that you are a newly appointed management consultant trainee and have received the following memo from your manager.

Memorandum

To: Trainee

From: Beverly Jones
Office Manager

We have received the above brief from Rainbow United Football Club and have been asked to prepare a report for the Board Meeting in two weeks' time. I would like you to tackle this case for me: it will be something for you to get your teeth into! I have arranged for you to visit the ground in two days' time so that you can gather any relevant and additional information you may require. After this can you carry out some research as set out below and produce a short informal report detailing all the information you have gathered under the headings: introduction, findings, conclusion.

---

1 Look at the information you are given about the Rainbow Football Club on the following pages. Comment on any **trends** you see occurring.

2 Analyse the **attendance and match receipts** for the two matches. What conclusions can you draw from this?

3 Analyse the **pricing policy** of the Football Club. Do you believe it can be improved in line with competitive teams or alternative sports?

Additional information

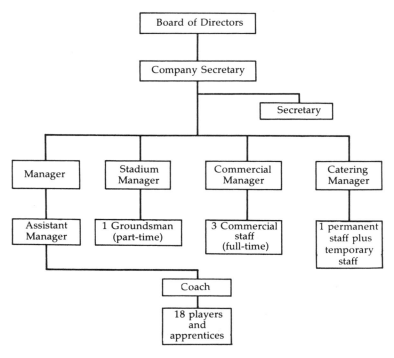

△ *Figure 13.1 Rainbow United Football Club organisation chart*

Revenue and costs for two matches in 19--

Rainbow United v. Amber United		Rainbow United v. Blue Foxes	
Gate: 1495 persons		Gate: 5107 persons	
Total Receipts: £2784.70		Total Receipts: £14 339	
Match Expenses:		*Match Expenses:*	
	£		£
Printing, Postage and Advertising	100.00	Printing, Postage and Advertising	100.00
Stewards/Gatekeepers	157.50	Stewards/Gatekeepers	177.00
Police	560.55	Police	560.55
Floodlighting	100.00	Floodlighting	100.00
VAT	417.71	VAT	2150.85
First Aid Staff	3.50	First Aid Staff	4.00
3% contribution to the Football League	71.01	3% contribution to the Football League	365.64

Notes

1 The 'Gate' refers to the number of people who attend the match and pay the standard entrance fees.

2 The contribution given to the Police is for crowd control.

3 The cost of the tickets to the public includes Value Added Tax (VAT) at 15 per cent. This has to be paid to the Inland Revenue by the Football Club.

4 The team is in Division 4 of the Football League and as such has to pay a contribution of 3 per cent of its match takings for this privilege. The 3 per cent is calculated on the takings after the VAT has been deducted.

5 The contribution for First Aid is a nominal sum given to the Red Cross organisation for allowing its volunteers to attend the matches.

Ticket prices for the 19--/19-- season

Blocks	Price	
Seated	Adults	Children/OAPs
A & G	£4.00	£2.00
B & F	£4.50	£2.25
C & D	£5.25	£2.60
Standing	£3.00	£1.50

Season tickets

Seated		
Blocks A, B, C, D, F, G	£80.00	£35.00
Standing	£50.00	£26.00

Note: The Blocks A, B, C, D, F, and G refer to the seating areas at the football ground. All the season tickets are priced at £80.00 and are sold on a 'first come first served' basis.

The summarised Trading and Profit and Loss Accounts for Rainbow United Football Club for the years ended 31 May 19-- and 31 May 19--.

	£	19-- £	£	19-- £
Turnover		443 000		498 000
Less:				
Playing and administration expenses	536 000		539 000	
Bank interest payable	30 000		27 000	
		566 000		566 000
Loss on ordinary activities for the year		(123 000)		(68 000)
Adverse profit and loss account balance brought forward (from previous year)		(212 000)		(144 000)
Adverse profit and loss account balance carried forward (to the Balance sheet for the respective years)		(335 000)		(212 000)

Notes

	£	£
1 *Turnover comprises:*		
Gate receipts	93 000	98 000
Football Association receipts	84 000	103 000
Transfer fees received	41 000	48 000
Commercial activities	217 000	232 000
Donations	8 000	17 000
	443 000	498 000
2 *Playing and administration expenses:*		
Playing	294 000	304 000
Ground	26 000	30 000
Administration	186 000	160 000
Audit fee	2 000	2 000
Depreciation	9 000	15 000
Transfer fees paid	5 000	22 000
Other	14 000	6 000
	536 000	539 000

Summarised Balance Sheets

		19--		19--
	£	£	£	£
Fixed assets		626 000		634 000
Current assets				
Debtors	67 000		66 000	
Stock	2 000		1 000	
Other	1 000		1 000	
	70 000		68 000	
Creditors	(342 000)		(298 000)	
Net current liabilities		(272 000)		(230 000)
Total net assets		354 000		404 000
Financed by:				
Capital and reserves		586 000		552 000
Profit and loss account		(335 000)		(212 000)
Long term liabilities		103 000		64 000
		354 000		404 000

Notes

1 The Profit and Loss Account Balance is the Balance Carried Forward from the Profit and Loss Accounts.

	19--	19--
	£	£
2 Long term liabilities are:		
Bank loan	53 000	64 000
Town Council loan	50 000	—
	103 000	64 000
3 Creditors are:		
Bank overdraft	130 000	167 000
Other creditors	212 000	131 000
	342 000	298 000

Table 13.2 Average attendances at football matches[1]

	Football League (England & Wales)				Scottish Football League		
	Division 1	Division 2	Division 3	Division 4	Premier Division	Division 1	Division 2
1961–62	26 106	16 132	9 419	6 060		11 178	1 686
1966–67	30 829	15 701	8 009	5 407		8 683	1 127
1971–72	31 352	14 652	8 510	4 981		5 228	564
1976–77	29 540	13 529	7 522	3 863	11 844	2 393	785
1980–81	24 660	11 202	6 590	3 082	9 777	2 260	625
1981–82	22 556	10 282	5 159	3 621	9 467	1 926	570
1982–83	20 120	10 768	5 333	2 812	10 332	1 785	529
1983–84	18 856	11 601	4 946	2 822	11 522	1 679	778
1984–85	21 129	8 725	4 832	2 519	10 832	1 344	690
1985–86	19 562	7 696	4 522	2 554	12 558	1 288	827
1986–87	19 794[2]	9 192[2]	4 404[2]	3 178[2]	11 721[3]	1 524[3]	662

1 League matches only

2 Includes attendances for promotion and relegation play-off matches which were introduced in the 1986–87 season

3 From the 1986–87 season the Premier and First divisions in Scotland comprised 12 teams against 10 and 14 respectively in earlier seasons

From *Social Trends 18* 1988
© Crown Copyright 1988

MARKET RESEARCH

Look at Table 13.2.

1 Is football a declining spectator sport? Write a report outlining your conclusions, using the Central Statistical Office publications to back up your findings.

2 Find out the reasons behind the statistics. This may involve conducting a market research survey in your area. The following notes may be of help in planning your questionnaire:
   a) Establish the market profile of people who visit/support your local football club or another professional club, and people who watch other spectator sports.
   b) Find out how often people attend local football club matches and other events which may be organised by the club. It might be useful to contrast this with attendance at other professional clubs' matches and other spectator sports.
   c) If people do not attend any events at the club find out why this is so.
   d) Find out what type of events people would like to see held at the club and which they would be prepared to support.
   e) Find out the public's opinion of the standard of facilities/variety of services and products offered by your club compared to other football clubs.
   f) Find out the public's opinion of the prices charged for various goods and services at your club.
   g) Who does not use the club?
   Include demographic data such as age, sex, occupation, socio-economic groupings, place of residence, etc. in your survey.

3 Using your local football club as an example, find out as much as possible about the following areas:
   a) The location of the club and the advantages and disadvantages of its location to members of the public, players, local residents, football supporters, local businesses and so on.
   b) The club's health and safety policy and fire precautions; are they adequate?
   c) Facilities and equipment in use at the club.
   d) Other commercial services offered by the club.
   e) Past fund-raising events/non-football events held by your club during the last year. Produce a detailed proposal for the organisation of one non-football event which could be organised in the future.
   f) Facilities and access available for disabled supporters of the club.
   g) Any marketing or promotional activity which is undertaken by the club.

4 You have been requested to submit a further report investigating the introduction of new technology into the sport of football.
   The following points should be covered:
   ● What new innovations are being used
   ● What economic and social benefits this will have for the staff, players and supporters of the football club
   ● The disadvantages of the introduction of this new technology to staff, players, supporters and the general public.

14 Design

Aims

▶ To look at principles of good and bad design in local leisure facilities
▶ To evaluate what the user appreciates in design of leisure amenities
▶ To investigate design elements and consider how they relate to the leisure industry

Principles of good design

You do not have to be an artist or a designer to appreciate design and the skills involved in visual discrimination. The phrase 'aesthetically pleasing' is often used to describe something that corresponds to the principles of good taste. When related to a leisure facility good design usually means something that appeals to the eye, is practical and durable, is easily cleaned and maintained and does not show signs of ageing a few months after being used.

The principles of design apply to the building as well as fixtures and fittings; e.g. the equipment, interior decor, facilities such as eating areas, showers and toilets, reception areas and noticeboards. Principles of good design do not only apply to built facilities such as sports and leisure centres, theatres and community centres, but also to outdoor facilities such as country parks, nature trails and water sports centres. It is just as important when managing a natural resource (such as an area designated as a national park) to include amenities which are well-designed – for example, signposts, way markers, resting places or hides, picnic areas and public conveniences – in order to enhance and prolong use by members of the public.

Consider the following example, based on a leisure centre. Does it seem familiar to you?

Example: the leisure centre

Imagine having to walk up two flights of concrete steps then queueing up to be admitted through a turnstile while you pay the entry money. The changing room is crowded, with no lockers and the stench of sweaty bodies makes you feel ill before you embark on your activity.

After putting your body through the torment of highly energetic physical activity (all in the name of fitness), you find that the shower alternates between hot and cold, with only a trickle of water anyway! Feeling ravenous and badly in need of liquid replenishment you drag yourself to the cafeteria, only to find that a stale uninviting cheese roll is all that remains and there is standing room only.

'What about me, the customer', you may think to yourself. 'I thought that sports centres were built for our pleasure!'

Fortunately most modern sports and leisure centres have been constructed with economy and customer comfort in mind. Let us then consider some of the recommendations made by the Sports Council regarding the design of standardised sports centres (which are referred to as SASH – Standardised Approach to Sports Halls).

Layout

The layout should be logical with inclusion of multiple use areas and curtains to section off areas. The use of space is important in order to give the impression of uncluttered surroundings. High ceilings and clear walkways can give a feeling of space even though this may be limited. Cramped and difficult-to-find facilities do not create a good impression.

Reception

The reception should provide a good view of the entrance hall in order to control access into the building. This can be the nerve centre of the building and may incorporate lighting control, public address outlet, telephone switchboard, booking facilities and hire of equipment.

Changing rooms

Changing rooms should be visible to staff and users, i.e. clearly marked. Communal or individual showers, or a mixture of both, are acceptable. Specialist changing facilities may be necessary for swimmers, disabled users, clubs, schools, family groups, or staff of the centre. Clean and comfortable changing conditions are important in encouraging the proper use of facilities.

Floors

The activity areas should ideally be wooden to absorb impact. Carpets should be used in certain areas to reduce noise, for example, in the corridors, eating and bar areas.

Interior decor

Colours should be appealing to the eye; reds, greens and dark blues tend to make a room appear smaller than it actually is, whereas lighter colours such as whites, greys, and beige give a more open impression. The use of colour in an interior is a very powerful medium and should be carefully chosen. In the past rich colours such as red and gold were used to promote the impression of splendour and brilliance (as in the Victorian theatres), however more neutral colours offer less distraction to the users. The inclusion of plants and natural vegetation serves to break up a 'clinical' or bare area and makes an area appear 'natural'. However plants need attention; if they are allowed to become unhealthy they create a run-down image of the amenity. Artificial greenery is often used in preference to real plants. Textures of floor and wall coverings and the interior decor of a building create an overall impression of the whole amenity. Thick carpets, textured wallpaper and thick velvet curtains give the impression of richness, but this may be entirely unsuitable for an activity area. The cleaning of floor and wall coverings and window curtains or blinds must also be considered.

▶
The leisure club
reception, Abbots Well
Hotel, Chester

Lighting

This should be of good quality, bearing in mind the different activity requirements and the direction of play for sport. Soft lighting is applicable to eating and relaxing areas, whereas brighter lighting is needed for activity areas. Lighting in spectator areas should not produce glare for either players or spectators. Security lighting is recommended outside the entrances and exits.

Windows

While it is desirable to have as much natural light as possible, windows are often small because of the advantages of reduced heating costs.

Heating

The type of heating used should be economical. Warm air heating is best for low cost schemes. A mechanical ventilation system will always be required to facilitate the movement of air. It is important that the facilities are not over-heated, although the changing rooms must be comfortably warm.

Social areas

Comfortable chairs, carpets and eating areas are important to encourage users to stay on the premises after their activities to socialise. The scale of refreshment facilities varies from vending machines, licensed bars and cafeterias to restaurants offering table service. If refreshment facilities are on the first floor, a lift or hoist should be provided in order that all users and visitors can benefit from the amenity.

Notice boards

It is important to think of the number of boards and their positioning; they need to be in a prominent position where they can be read easily by users and visitors without causing disruption in corridors and reception areas.

Health and safety

Fire extinguishers, fire doors, fire alarms and emergency lighting are necessary. Fire exits should be well lit, and there should be guards over light fittings.

First aid room

These facilities should be available at all times.

Storage areas

These must be large enough to hold equipment which should be easily accessible.

Maintenance areas

These are desirable for repairing and cleaning equipment.

Offices

Often these are open plan with screens for privacy and to cut down noise levels. Plants and carpets also contribute to the establishment of a conducive pleasant working environment. There should be adequate storage for files and paperwork and a built-in night safe for cash and valuables.

Car parking

Free car parking close to the centre is a selling point. It is important to have disabled parking near the entrance, with ramps over the kerbs for wheelchair access.

Dual use centres

Community facilities should be recognisable by the public with information on display about classes, activities and so on. It is preferable to have separate entrances, storage areas and furniture for school and community use because users from the community may feel inhibited by groups of school pupils or college students using the same facilities.

1 Visit your local leisure facility and write a report on the facilities using the above criteria as guidelines.

2 During your visit pick up any leaflets aimed at different user groups and look carefully at the notice boards. Compile a list of the various user groups and the facilities provided for them, e.g. housewives: women's mornings; offering a range of activities; crèche provided.

3 Analyse the design of sports or leisure facility that you use. How user-friendly is it?

The second example concerns theatre design.

Example: the theatre

Theatre design has changed radically from the days when watching plays became popular in Elizabethan England. Originally 'apron front' stages, the lack of elevated seating and viewing pit where people stood (amongst rowdy audiences) made the whole experience a rather 'down-market' activity, attempted only if you were interested in the seamier side of life.

It was not until the Restoration period and during the reign of Charles II that play-watching became a more orderly affair, although the Lord Chamberlain sought to regulate the quality and nature of the performance. In the Victorian era theatres took on a new lease of life, inspired by better design and seating arrangements. To watch a performance 'up in the gods' was to view it from afar in the gallery, although your view might well be obscured by a pillar!

In modern times the design of purpose-built theatres has been improved. Revolving stages are used for efficient set changing, and the use of technology ensures very realistic backdrops and scenery. There is adequate storage space and well-appointed dressing rooms with showers and rest areas.

For the patrons there are computerised booking facilities and, once inside, rows of tiered seats for comfort which give a clear view of the stage from almost anywhere in the house. The acoustics are good and the sound systems usually good enough for even the hard of hearing to appreciate what the actors are saying. Disabled patrons are encouraged by purpose-built facilities and removable chairs. Often the theatre can be used for a variety of other purposes such as a cinema, concert hall, or opera house, and may include community facilities such as exhibition galleries, bar and restaurant.

Outside, adequate car-parking facilities ensures there is little problem with people arriving late and fewer queues of cars after the performance. Theatre-going has become a pleasure and a 'civilised' entertainment, mainly due to design improvements over recent years.

The economic theatre
Look at the plan of the theatre in Figure 14.1, page 156. This amenity was designed in the 1930s and has doubled as a theatre and a cinema up to the present day. At present a Trust administers the theatre and it was refurbished in the early 1960s. Now the Trust is hoping that a donor will provide 350 new seats, the old seats having become worn and creaking after 30 years of wear and tear!

From looking at the plan and visiting the theatre the following points were noted:

● It was difficult to see the stage from the back of either the gallery or the stalls. Binoculars were supplied for patrons.
● The seating is at different angles at the sides of the stalls and balcony in order to maximise the audience's view of the stage.

- The space between the seats is very limited (the seats themselves are immovable), so anyone taller than 5'7" is at an immediate disadvantage and will become uncomfortable during a performance.
- There is no built-in microphone for the players on the stage who must project their voices adequately in order to be heard at the back.
- The stage is inflexible and, in order for scenery to be changed without the audience watching the curtains have to be drawn.
- There is very limited access for the physically disabled or wheelchair-bound patrons. There are no ramps, and fixed seating means that a wheelchair would have to be placed in the aisle.
- There are very few signposts of facilities such as the bar and toilets.
- Fire exits and doors are not marked on the plan, but these are clearly signed in the actual premises.
- There are no car-parking facilities in the vicinity of the theatre so patrons have to walk from the nearest municipal car park which is about a ten-minute walk, or try to find car-parking spaces on the side streets.

Visit your local theatre or cinema and find out about its design. Can you suggest any improvements?

SEATING PLAN

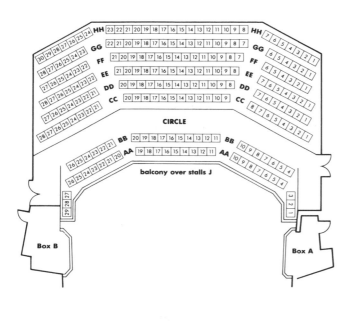

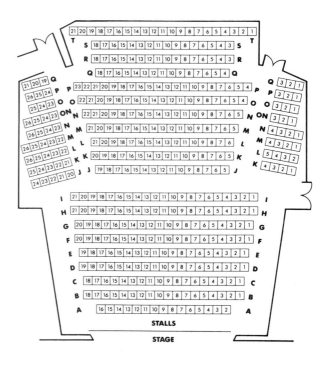

▲ *Figure 14.1   The Economic Theatre; seating plan*

Outdoor leisure facilities

These have to be managed and certain aspects have to be designed by the organisation that runs the amenity, so that all potential users have maximum enjoyment of the area. For instance, a nature trail in a waste area of a city should be signposted, have adequate rubbish bins in any picnic area, exhibit warning signs if any part of the area is dangerous and offer alternative routes to elderly, infirm or disabled users.

If little thought or effort has been given in designing routes and amenities, then only certain user groups will use the facility and it may be costly to maintain. For example, if no rubbish bins are provided in a picnic area litter will have a detrimental effect on the area, decreasing popularity with users and provoking legal problems with local residents and local councils. The cost of maintaining and servicing the rubbish bins is less than the potential cost of legal fees, decline in membership and damage to the environment.

ACTIVITY

1 Visit one of the following in your area:

- A local Wildlife Trust Nature Trail
- A Royal Society for the Protection of Birds (RSPB) Reserve
- A National Trust Park
- A local authority 'Trim Trail'
- Any organised and managed outdoor activity place.

2 Make a list of all the aspects of the amenity that have to be designed, e.g. public conveniences, sign posts, etc.

3 Could the design of the amenity be improved from a user's point of view? If so, how?

Corporate image

The design world includes many specialists who are consulted when advice is needed. They range from interior designers, fashion consultants, and specialist designers such as craftsmen, engineers, etc. These people, through their practical knowledge and ability, can contribute to the major success or failure of a project.

In particular, an organisation's corporate image must be easily recognisable and durable enough to stand the test of time and competition. Organisations often adopt a **logo** which is an instantly recognisable symbol (e.g. the Sports Council logo, see page 43) and it uses this to increase the public's awareness of its activities. In the same way a **uniform** is part of an organisation's corporate image; it is a distinctive mode of dress adopted by those involved in an organisation and draws attention to the organisation itself.

Consider the following:

An early morning TV article (April 1990)

'Concern has been expressed by the organisers over the unattractive uniform, falling enrolment, increasing alternative activities and the ability of girls to join the Scout movement. This has resulted in falling membership numbers of the Guides; a trend likely to continue unless something is done to increase the attractiveness of this once popular movement.'

The organisers of the Guides decided that the movement needed an updated public image. To start the process of change they called in Jeff Banks, the fashion designer, to design a new uniform which would be more practical for the activities undertaken, and to launch them into the twenty-first century. His brief was to make the uniform as attractive, practical and durable as possible, bearing in mind that it could not be too expensive and not so fashionable that it dated too quickly. The result was pleasing and should help the movement so that it does not become outdated.

► *A new look for the Guides*

For whom the bathing bells toll

by Daphne Glazer

The secret place where I love to spend Saturday afternoons or some stolen lunch hours is under threat.

Beverley Road swimming baths in Hull is like no other. The moment I see the handsome brick face with its green onion domes, and push open the heavy doors, I'm expectant. Curly green leaves and blue and red flowers twine in leaded lights in the half-glass doors. The floor in the foyer is mosaic. There are bluish-green art nouveau tiles running along the walls, and all the door handles are brass and marked by distinctive art nouveau curlicues.

I get my ticket at the pay desk and then I'm walking across the hall and through a further pair of half-glass doors and the pool is lying before me. It's a lovely blue and is flanked by changing cubicles. Above me is a glassed-in roof, and a balcony decorated by attractive iron scrolling runs round the bath.

There is no nonsense about putting clothes

in mesh baskets and trundling round to lockers which won't lock or for which you have to have 10p coins when you've only got 5p coins. No, you can leave your clothes in the cubicle and plunge straight into the gleaming surface.

With the sunlight glancing down and forming blobby patterns on the water, swimming conjures up tropical islands or exotic conservatories filled with thick-leaved green, twining plants. Outside the pavements may be covered with a scum of ice, but inside the baths the steam rises mysteriously and hangs over the swimmers as they glide up and down the lengths.

The atmosphere changes depending on the time of day. During the over-fifties sessions, bands of ladies in pink, white or blue caps huddle at the shallow end and gossip about operations and grandchildren, while groups of gentlemen perform strange snorkling exercises and porpoise up the bath, rising occasionally to gulp in lungfuls of air. There is a Roman bath, leisured feel to the occasion. Swimming is only part of the total experience.

During sessions designated as public, the clientele is more varied, but all are known to one another. Shoals of tadpoley boys nose dive and wind you as they surface. Youths with hearts and daggers, and Mam And Dad, inscribed on their arms in blue and red, wrestle and do breath-taking dives, or canoodle with girls whose bathing costumes vanish into the cracks of their bottoms.

I have seen one lady progress from flapping about with orange armbands in the shallow end to ploughing a stately furrow up and down the bath, head erect, spectacles on, white bath cap pulled well down. "Well, you see," she confided in the showers, "I'm 75 and I had this dream that I was swimming. I could feel it . . . feel myself gliding, and it was wonderful and I thought, I want to do that. Mind you, I couldn't swim then – always been afraid of water. I told my daughter and she said, 'Mam, you must learn.' And so I have: 70 lengths I do now. It's like I saw it in my dream."

All this is about to change, and why? Beverley Road baths has been open since 1891. In the 40s and 50s it was used in winter as a dance hall. Recently, snippets in the local paper announced that the swimming pool would have to close down as it would be too expensive to repair. After public protest meetings and petitions, there was a reprieve. The baths would be renovated.

The news leaked out that the original pool was to be shortened and the site developed into a modern leisure centre. The latest word is that the present pool is to be removed as it would cost £3 million to repair it. It is proposed to build a new bath on the lines of a leisure centre which has already been put up in another part of the town. This, it is alleged, would be much cheaper. As the facade is listed, it will remain untouched.

I feel outraged that this historic building may be gutted in favour of a "modern leisure centre". We already have several of these in Hull and its environs. They are concrete boxes with wave machines and shortened pools which are not really intended for serious swimming. There is about them an ugly utilitarian quality; they also tend to be very expensive for ordinary people to use. In a few years' time, these shoddy structures will be pulled down.

Here is another instance of the throwaway society which Toffler foresaw 20 years ago. Our growing emphasis on profit making in all areas of life will only intensify the trend.

"Why can't Beverley Road baths be repaired?", I continue to ask. "You can't expect the ratepayer to fork out that much," I was told by a local politician. "It won't be economic." How does he know what the ratepayer's reaction might be? Public opinion is not being consulted. If it were the case that a city like Hull can't afford such repairs, surely there should be a central government fund to assist a city which wants to preserve some building of historic interest but would find itself under financial pressure were it to do so?

According to my latest observations, the plot thickens even further. I enquired at the baths if I might take a few photographs of the interior. "You'll have to ask the director of leisure services," came the reply.

Someone on the telephone in the office of the director said: "I'm afraid you can't do that. You'd need to make a formal request in writing to the director – and I'm not sure you'd be allowed to even then. . . ."

"What on earth is this?" I asked, beginning to wonder whether I had inadvertently wandered into high-security territory.

"When the baths goes private in April, it's going to be up for tender . . . we can't have people taking photographs before that."

What does this mean? Now, every time I push open those doors, I feel a certain apprehension. Will this be my last swim there? Can anything hold the bulldozers back?

Article from *The Guardian*, 9 February 1990

Read the article 'For whom the bathing bells toll'.

1 Answer the following questions related to the design:
   a) When was the pool originally built and in what style?
   b) Do you think that the pool is suitable for its use today? Give reasons for your answer.
   c) What opinion has the writer on the design and continued use of the pool?
   d) What design problems are there in allowing a purpose-built Victorian swimming pool to operate today?
   e) What are the major criticisms the writer has of modern leisure centres?

2 Using the leisure map you completed of your area in Chapter 3 (Assignment 2) identify any purpose-built Victorian buildings that are still in use today (for the same purpose for which they were built). Visit the amenity and draw up a report. The report should include the following:
   a) Any changes you believe have been made in the structure of the building to enhance its use in the twentieth century.
   b) An identification of any areas of design which you believe are inappropriate for its continued use today.

Optional facilities

(See pages 162 and 163 for plans of the SASH options.)

Squash courts

The SASH squash courts link to an extension of the main corridor. Externally the squash courts match the main building and internally their finishes are of a high and functional standard approved by the Squash Rackets Association. The Sports Hall changing facilities are sufficient to cope with the demand generated by up to six squash courts, and additional changing space can be provided if necessary.

Glass back viewing walls are standard, and an optional high-level viewing gallery with seats above and below can be provided.

It is also now possible to incorporate a sliding side wall between double courts to create an ancillary space for non-squash court activities such as aerobics, crèche or coaching sessions.

Ancillary hall

The SASH Ancillary Hall can be constructed to a modular size and height to meet individual clients' requirements and is ideal for many indoor sports including table tennis, boxing, fencing, judo, karate, wrestling, bowls and keep-fit.

The Ancillary Hall can also be designed and fitted-out to create a community centre, performing arts theatre, and cater for a wide range of local exhibitions and leisure activities while still maintaining the flexibility for sporting use.

Swimming pool

The SASH leisure pool and its modern, attractive design, promotes an exciting yet relaxing atmosphere. It is highly insulated and comprehensively equipped and it features the latest water purification systems, efficient acoustics and economy of operation.

The SASH swimming pool contains both main and learner pools and is constructed to the same exacting design and specification.

SASH Internal options

SASH now offers a limited range of internal layout and usage options and can be enhanced with additional facilities.

These include mat store, sauna, solarium, crèche, coaching room and enlarged bar area.

The first floor can also be adapted to create additional office space, committee room and viewing screen to main hall.

▲ SASH specification for Assignment 15

Summary

▶ Good design is an extremely important element to any leisure facility. It can improve the enjoyment of the facility for users and promote membership.

▶ Elements of bad design have far reaching repercussions, e.g. loss of popularity with users, health and safety problems, legal wrangles and so on.

▶ Design needs to be considered carefully and if possible discussed with experts such as interior designers, safety officers, engineers and so on. This ensures that the facility conforms not only to good taste and is pleasing to the eye, but is structurally sound and potentially safe.

▶ Simple design skills are easily learnt, for instance, the use of space, shape, colour, and texture. These are fun to experiment with and can give insight into how people perceive products, services and the environment.

Assignment 15

DESIGN A LEISURE CENTRE

1 Select a leisure facility in your area and produce a scaled plan using graph paper. Indicate the position of doors, windows and walls. Look again at the essential criteria for sports halls and assess each of the categories below, using a scale of 1 to 6 (where 1 equals Very Poor and 6 equals Excellent).
   a) Size/layout and floors
   b) Interior decor/lighting and heating
   c) Customer services/reception, changing rooms, bar/cafe facilities
   d) Publicity leaflets and noticeboards
   e) Safety procedure and equipment and first aid provision
   f) Maintenance and storage areas
   g) Hygiene and cleanliness

If possible get others in your group to do this exercise. You can then compare the total number of points awarded.

Assume you are a user of the facility and write a letter to the manager summarising your evaluation and making any suitable recommendations.

2 Assume you are Assistant Sports and Recreation Officer for the local authority in your area. The council (local authority) is proposing to build a new sports centre and you have received the following memo from your boss. Refer to the SASH optional facilities on page 160 and diagrams on pages 162 and 163.

Memorandum

To: Assistant Sports and Recreation Officer
From: Sports and Recreation Officer

I have just received an invitation to a meeting with the architects of the proposed Sports Centre. The Centre is to be a SASH Centre, as it is being partially funded by the Sports Council. The object of the meeting is for me to express my views on the particular facilities/options we would recommend to meet the needs of the local community. Can you get hold of the Sports Council SASH guidelines and give me your opinion in a report by the end of next week.

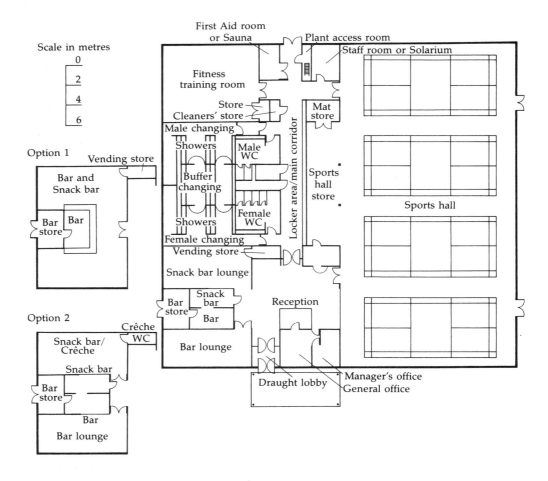

Scale in metres

0
2
4
6

First Aid room or Sauna

Plant access room

Staff room or Solarium

Fitness training room

Store

Cleaners' store

Male changing

Showers

Male WC

Buffer changing

Female WC

Showers

Female changing

Vending store

Snack bar lounge

Mat store

Sports hall store

Locker area/main corridor

Sports hall

Option 1

Vending store

Bar and Snack bar

Bar store

Bar

Bar store

Snack bar

Bar

Reception

Bar lounge

Option 2

Crèche WC

Snack bar/ Crèche

Snack bar

Bar store

Bar

Bar lounge

Draught lobby

Manager's office

General office

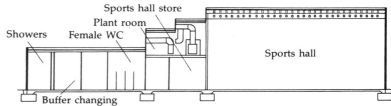

Sports hall store

Plant room

Showers

Female WC

Sports hall

Buffer changing

▲ *SASH design for sports centre A (Assignment 15)*

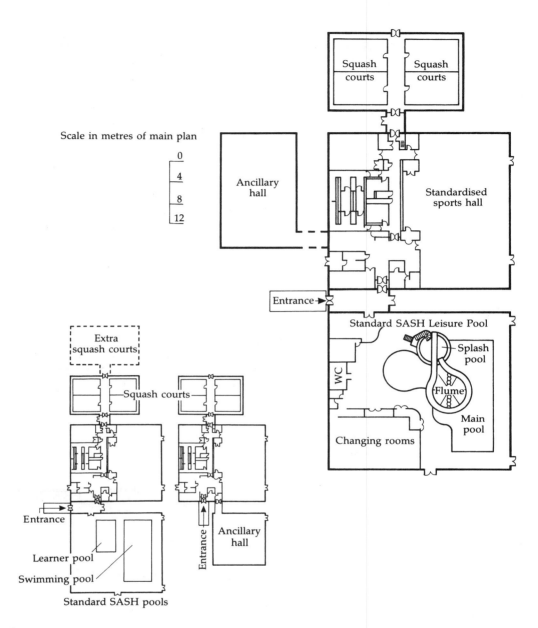

Scale in metres of main plan

0
4
8
12

Squash courts

Squash courts

Ancillary hall

Standardised sports hall

Entrance →

Standard SASH Leisure Pool

WC

Splash pool

Flume

Main pool

Changing rooms

Extra squash courts

Squash courts

Entrance →

Entrance ↑

Ancillary hall

Learner pool

Swimming pool

Standard SASH pools

▲ *SASH design for sports centre B (Assignment 15)*

Appendix 1

Index of leisure and sports activities

abseiling
acrobatics
aerobics
aeronautics
angling
animal keeping/breeding
apiculture
archaeology
aromatherapy
astrology
astronomy
athletics

backpacking
ball games
ballooning
beer making
bingo playing
blood sports
BMX riding
board games
boating
body building
body surfing
botany
boule
bowls
boxing
brass rubbing
building (anything)
busking

cake icing/decoration
calligraphy
callisthenics
camping
campanology
candle making
canoeing
card playing
caravanning
carnivals
car maintenance and restoration
cartography
cartooning
carving

caving
charades
choristry
choreography
church going
cinema going
circuit training
circus visiting
clay model making
clay pigeon shooting
climbing
clock making
collecting (anything, e.g. bottles, coins, vintage cars)
computer games
cooking
creative writing
cricket
crochet
croquet
cruising
curling
cycling

dancing (disco, ballroom, jazz, morris, barn, etc.)
dart playing
dining out
discus
dog racing/showing/walking
do it yourself (DIY)
doll making/repair
dominoes
drama
dress making
dressing up
driftwood collecting/polishing
driving
dungeons and dragons
dwile flonking

education
egg painting
elocution

embroidery
entertaining
equestrian eventing
expeditions
exploring

faith healing
falconry
farriery
fell walking/running
fencing
ferret keeping
film making
fish breeding
fishing
flat racing
flower arranging/pressing
folk singing
french polishing
fruit picking
furniture making

gambling
gardening
geneaology
glass blowing
gliding
go-karting
golf
gold digging
grand prix racing
gurning
gymnastics

hammer throwing
hang gliding
heptathlon
heraldry
herbalism
herpatology
high jump
holidaying
homeopathy
holography
hospital visiting
hurling
hypnotism

ice climbing
ice hockey
ice skating
impersonating
indoor athletics
indoor sports

jam making
javelin
jewellery making
jogging
joinery
jousting
judo
juggling
jumble sale visiting

keep fit
kick boxing
kite flying
knitting

lace making
lamp making
language learning
land yachting
letter writing
long bow shooting
long distance running
long jump

magical arts
majorettes
manicures
massage
martial arts
matchstick model building
meals on wheels
meditation
metal detecting
meteorology
miming
model making
motocross
motorcar racing
motor boat racing
mountaineering
mud wrestling
music (performing,
    listening, etc.)

naturism
needlework
night clubbing

opera going
orienteering
origamy
ornithology

pageantry
painting
palaeobotany
palaeography
palaeontology
palmistry
paper chasing
parascending
parachuting
paragliding
party going
patchwork quilt making
people watching
pentathlon
photography
picnicking
pigeon fancying
pigeon racing
pistol shooting
philately
philosophy
plane spotting
poetry
pole vaulting
politics
polo
pony trekking
pooh sticks
pool
potholing
pottery
prison visiting
public speaking
puning

quarry racing
questing
quilt making
quoits

raft racing
rally racing
rambling
racquet sports
reading
religion
riding
roller skating
rowing
rug making

safaris
sailing
sauna
scuba diving
sculling
sculpture

seaside visiting
sewing
shooting
shopping
sign writing
singing
song writing
sketching
ski-ing
skate boarding
snooker
snorkelling
soccer
softball
solarium
squash
stock car racing
Subbuteo
sun bathing
surfing
swimming
swogging
synchronised swimming

table football
table tennis
tai quondo
tapestry
target shooting
tarot card reading
tatting
tattoing
tea leaf reading
television watching
tennis
ten pin bowling
Thai boxing
theatre going
theme park visiting
three-legged racing
tiddlywinks
toxophily
toxology
toy making
train spotting
trampolining
trap driving
trekking
triathlon
tug of war
tunnel exploring

umpiring
uni-cycling
upholstery

varnishing
venture scouting
video watching/making
vine growing
visiting (e.g. friends,
    galleries, monuments,
    museums)

walking

watch mending
water sports
weight lifting
weight watchers
welly throwing
window shopping
windsurfing
wine making

wine tasting
wrestling
wrought-iron work
writing

yachting
yoga

zoo visiting

Appendix 2

Roles for Dry Ski Slope, Assignment 4, pages 63–4

Conservative councillors (3)
You are in favour of the scheme because it encourages private enterprise and there is a lack of leisure amenities in the town. The scheme will also help the tourism trade, which boosts the local economy. You have to be careful because many of the Springfield residents are conservative supporters and you do not want to upset them.

Labour councillors (3)
You are against the scheme because although there is a shortage of leisure amenities, you do not feel that locals will benefit personally as ski-ing is an 'exclusive' sport. Many of your supporters do not have enough disposable income to benefit from this and are unlikely to be going on ski-ing holidays, which are very much 'up-market'. You would prefer private money to be invested in a new leisure centre, which would benefit the whole community.

Independent councillor A
You are against the scheme because of the environmental issues. Many of the environmental lobbyists are in your Ward.

Independent councillor B
You are for the scheme because you have had a lot of positive response from your ward, where there are a lot of young people living. You are also a full-time lecturer at the local further education college and feedback from the students has been very positive.

Independent councillor C
You are undecided and can see both points of view.

Lobbyists
You are members of Greenpeace and are very concerned about wildlife and precious plant life in the area. You think that the area should be established as Green Belt territory. Additionally, according to a local historian, it is one of the most historic sites in the city as it was once a Roman burial ground with an Iron Age fort.

Local residents
You are worried about the traffic congestion, and the effect on house prices, which are expected to decline. Also the noise element and rowdyism are perturbing issues, together with the increase in crime rate which is to be expected.

Business developers
You feel that it would be good for tourism and the local residents. Your market research has revealed that it is an affluent area and that it is a viable proposition. Moreover, research has shown that at peak times no more than 40 cars will use the road leading to the complex. Dry slope skiing is a sport that can be enjoyed independently of snow skiing and your plans will include something for everyone in the Leisure Pursuits Park. Other local businesses would reap the benefits of this development, e.g. the shops and pubs and restaurants and possibly the hotels and guest-houses too. The locals will be able to use the bar without charge. Membership will be £2.50 for day membership, or £100 per year which includes access to all the facilities, apart from skiing. This will be charged at £4 per hour and £1.50 for the hire of all skis, boots and sticks.

Student representatives

You are for the scheme as there is little for young people to do in the town.

Mayor

You are the chairperson and must direct the meeting to ensure that everyone gets a chance to express their opinion equally. Whilst the meeting is in progress, make notes of the advantages and disadvantages of the scheme and read them out before calling for the vote. **NB:** The mayor has the casting vote, should this be necessary.

Journalists

You are looking for a story for the front page of today's local paper and are very keen to identify the controversial issues.

Roles for West Winton Tennis Club Activity, page 85

Treasurer

You are worried that the social events incur debts. The last time a disco was held it was not a success and a loss of £50.00 was made. Suggest increasing the cost of membership and coaching charges to members.

Assistant Treasurer

You are also worried about the income and expenditure of the Club but believe social fund raising events do work, if properly managed.

Chairperson

You must keep the meeting in order and try to reach a decision acceptable to the majority at the end of the meeting. You are responsible for summarising the points made at the meeting and are allowed a casting vote in the event of a stalemate situation at the end of the meeting.

Secretary

You usually take the minutes of a meeting, but have no voting rights. You are very sociable, with some good suggestions for outdoor fund raising events, such as a barbeque, sponsored fun run and a disco. (The local community centre can be hired at the nominal charge of £5.00 per evening.)

Fixtures Secretary

You are worried about the time spent raising money and in the past have found it very difficult to get teams together and organise league events. Consequently the club did not do well in the league. You prefer club members to concentrate on playing tennis rather than turning it into a glorified social club.

Coach

You need the tennis courts to be in good working order and up to standard. You believe that the club may well lose good potential players to rival clubs who have better facilities. You are willing to undertake coaching at nominal fees, believing that young members must be given the opportunity to develop their potential.

Junior Representative

You are worried that if a social event is arranged it will not be the type of event that younger members might like to support. You want to stage an event that will appeal to the under-16s.

Club Members

You have a variety of ideas for the club fund-raising activities and suggest ideas for future policy of the club and its facilities.

Roles for Managing People Problems, Assignment 9, page 119

Role play 1

Employee: You are a receptionist in a leisure centre. Recently one of the male customers has been harrassing you and has made sexual innuendos. You have tried to be polite and cool but he is still persistent. He is 20 years older than you and has a wife and three children. Now you have had enough and want to complain to the manager. You think that the customer should be banned from using the club . . .

Manager: You are the manager of a leisure club and the receptionist has asked to see you about a problem with a male customer. This customer is a friend of yours. You know he is rather loud-mouthed and a bit of a womaniser but he is harmless in your opinion.

Role play 2

Manager: You are manager of a private health club and have received complaints about one of the squash coaches. She has been running a beginners' course but customers complain that she is impatient and condescending. She is of county playing standard and is currently taking a coaching qualification.

Employee: You are a part-time squash coach at a health club, are of county playing standard and are taking a squash qualification. You are currently coaching a beginners' class which you enjoy, but you find it difficult to get back to basics and you get rather nervous while coaching. Your manager has asked to see you . . .

Role play 3

Manager: You are manager of a leisure centre and have had complaints about one of the supervisors who has been slipping off early and has not been pulling his/her weight recently. This is rather uncharacteristic behaviour. You have asked to speak to him/her.

Employee: You are a supervisor in a sports hall and have been rather depressed recently because your wife/husband has been very ill. You have tried to slip home as often as possible without anyone noticing. Your manager has asked to see you . . .

Role play 4

Manager: You are the manager of a leisure centre. Three times in the past fortnight the bar till has been down by £5–10. There are two barpersons. One has worked there for several years and you are sure that he/she is trustworthy. The new barperson started six weeks ago. You ask to see him/her.

Employee: You are a new barperson at the leisure centre and get on well with the other barperson who has worked there for years. He/she has told you that he/she would like to buy a house but their partner is unemployed so it will be difficult to afford a mortgage. The manager has asked to see you . . .

Appendix 3

Bibliography

Batterham, G. and Bishert, R. *et al*, *Administration of Leisure and Recreation Services*, Kingston upon Thames: Croner Publications, 1989

Brailsford, D., *Sport and Society*, Routledge & Kegan Paul, 1969

Brighton Marina Village Harbour Guide, Sussex: Dawes Publishing, 1989

Byrne, T., *Local Government in Britain*, Middlesex: Penguin Books, 1983

Central Statistical Office, *Family Expenditure Survey*, Her Majesty's Stationery Office, 1985

Central Statistical Office, *Household Survey*, Her Majesty's Stationery Office, 1986

Central Statistical Office, *Regional Trends*, Her Majesty's Stationery Office, 1989

Central Statistical Office, *Social Trends*, Her Majesty's Stationery Office, 1989

Clark, J. and Critcher, C., *The Devil Makes Work: Leisure in Capitalist Britain*, London: Macmillan Publishers, 1985

Department of the Environment, *Developing Sport and Leisure*, Her Majesty's Stationery Office, 1989

Greenwood, J. and Wilson, D., *Public Administration in Britain*, London: George Allen & Unwin, 1984

Handbook of Tourism & Leisure, (CRAC), Hobsons Publishing PLC, 1989

Haywood, L., Kew, F. and Bramham, P., *Understanding Leisure*, London: Century Hutchinson, 1989

ILAM, *Leisure Management*, Vol. 9, No. 5, 1989

ILAM and the Sports Council, *Careers Opportunities in the Leisure Industry*, Sports Council, revised 1990

ILAM *The Leisure Manager*, 1989

Kennedy, D. and P., *Sport*, B. T. Batsford, 1975

Key British Enterprises, Dunn & Bradstreet, 1989

Malcolmson, R. W., *Popular Recreations in English Society*, Cambridge: Cambridge University Press, 1973

Martin, W. H. and Mason, S., *Broad Patterns of Leisure Expenditure*, London: The Sports Council and Social Science Research Council, 1983

Mecca PLC Careers and Education pack, 1989

Municipal Year Book, 1989

National Trust, *Annual Report*, membership magazines, various pamphlets

Office of Population Censuses and Surveys, *General Household Survey*, Her Majesty's Stationery Office, 1986

Parker, S. R., *Work and Leisure: Trends and Prospects*, London: The Sports Council and Social Science Research Council, 1980

Patmore, J. A., *Recreation and Resources*, Oxford: Basil Blackwell, 1983

Richards, S. G., *Introduction to British Government*, London, The Macmillan Press, 1983

Sceats, A., *Sports & Leisure Club Management*, Macdonald & Evans, 1985

Smith, S. L. J., *Recreation Geography*, Harlow: Longman, 1983

Sports Council, *Annual Report*, 1988/9

Sports Council, *Recreation Management*, Dartford: Janssen Services, 1989

Sports Council, *Sport in the Community; the next ten years*, 1982

Sports Council, *Standardised Approach to Sports Halls; Design Guide*, 1982

Stockdale, J. E., *What is Leisure?* London: The Sports Council and Economic & Social Research Council, 1985

Torkildsen, G.,*Leisure and Recreation Management*, E. & F. N. Spon Ltd, 1986

Walvin, J., *Leisure and Society 1830–1950*, Harlow: Longman, 1978

Wright, J., *Recreation and Leisure*, Kingston upon Thames: Croner Publications, 1989

Appendix 4

Useful addresses

The Arts Council (The Arts Council of Great Britain)
105 Piccadilly,
London W1V 0AU

British Tourist Authority
Thames Tower,
Black's Road,
Hammersmith,
London W6 9EL

The Central Council of Physical Recreation (CCPR)
Francis House,
Francis Street,
London SW1P 1DE

The Countryside Commission
John Dower House,
Crescent Place,
Cheltenham,
Gloucestershire GL50 3RA

English Heritage
(Historic Buildings and Monuments Commission for England)
Fortress House,
23 Saville Row,
London W1X 2HE

English Tourist Board
Thames Tower,
Black's Road,
Hammersmith,
London W6 9EL

The Forestry Commission
Headquarters,
231 Corstorphine Road,
Edinburgh EH12 7AT

The National Playing Fields Association
25 Ovington Square,
London SW3 1LQ

National Sports Centres
Crystal Palace NSC
Norwood,
London SE19 2BB

Bisham Abbey NSC,
Nr. Marlow,
Buckinghamshire
SL7 1RT

Lilleshall NSC,
Nr. Newport,
Shropshire
TF10 9AT

Holme Pierrepont National Water SC
Adbolton Lane,
Holme Pierrepont,
Nottingham NG12 2LU

Plas y Brenin National Centre for Mountain Activities
Capel Curig,
Gwynedd,
North Wales
LL24 0ET

The Royal Society for the Protection of Birds
The Lodge
Sandy
Bedfordshire
SG19 2DL

Sports Council
Head Office
16 Upper Woburn Place,
London WC1H 0QP

Regional Sports Councils
Northern Region
(Northumberland, Cumbria, Durham, Cleveland and Tyne and Wear)
Aykley Heads,
Durham DH1 5UU

North West Region
(Lancashire, Cheshire, Greater Manchester and Merseyside)
Astley House,
Quay Street,
Manchester M3 4AE

Yorkshire and Humberside
(West Yorkshire, South Yorkshire, North Yorkshire and Humberside)
Coronet House,
Queen Street,
Leeds LS1 4PW

East Midland Region
(Derbyshire, Nottinghamshire, Lincolnshire, Leicestershire and Northamptonshire)
Grove House,
Bridgeford Road,
West Bridgeford,
Nottingham NG2 6AP

West Midlands Region
(West Midlands, Hereford and Worcester, Shropshire, Staffordshire and Warwickshire)
Metropolitan House,
1 Hagley Road,
Five Ways, Edgbaston,
Birmingham B16 8TT

Eastern Region
(Norfolk, Cambridgeshire, Suffolk, Bedfordshire, Hertfordshire and Essex)
26–8 Bromham Road,
Bedford MK40 2QP

Greater London and South East Region
(Greater London, Surrey, Kent, East and West Sussex)
PO Box 480,
Crystal Palace National Sports Centre,
Ledrington Road,
London SE19 2BQ

South Western Region
(Avon, Cornwall, Devon, Dorset, Somerset, Wiltshire and Gloucestershire)
Ashlands House,
Ashlands,
Crewkerne,
Somerset TA18 7LQ

Index